GRAIN DUST
DREAMS

GRAIN DUST
DREAMS

DAVID W. TARBET

excelsior editions

AN IMPRINT OF STATE UNIVERSITY OF NEW YORK PRESS

Cover: Charles Demuth, 1883–1935
My Egypt, 1927
35¹⁵/₁₆ x 30 in. (91.3 x 76.2 cm)
Whitney Museum of American Art, New York; purchase, with funds from
Gertrude Vanderbilt Whitney 31.172
Digital Image © Whitney Museum of American Art

Published by State University of New York Press, Albany

Excelsior Editions is an imprint of State University of New York Press

For information, contact State University of New York Press, Albany, NY
www.sunypress.edu

Production, Ryan Morris
Marketing, Kate R. Seburyamo

Library of Congress Cataloging-in-Publication Data

Tarbet, David W., 1941–
    Grain dust dreams / David W. Tarbet.
        pages cm
    Includes bibliographical references and index.
    ISBN 978-1-4384-5816-8 (pbk. : alk. paper)
    ISBN 978-1-4384-5818-2 (e-book)
    1. Grain trade—New York (State)—Buffalo—History.   2. Grain trade—
Ontario—Thunder Bay—History.   3. Grain elevators—New York (State)—
Buffalo—Employees—History.   4. Grain elevators—Ontario—Thunder
Bay—Employees—History.   I. Title.
    HD9038.B9T37 2015
    338.1'7310971312—dc23   2014045150

10 9 8 7 6 5 4 3 2 1

Dedicated

to

my father

George Barclay Tarbet

Who worked many years in Thunder Bay's Manitoba Pool 1

Contents

Illustrations

Foreword

This book about grain elevators combines three elements: two geographic and one personal. The cities of Buffalo, New York, and Thunder Bay, Ontario, each, at different times, held the title of the world's greatest grain shipping port. They've earned their place in any book about terminal elevators. These aren't the only cities with grain elevators, of course. What connects them is my personal experience, that is, the fact that I've lived in both. I was born in Port Arthur, Ontario, and grew up in the twin city of Fort William. These two cities on the north shore of Lake Superior combined in 1970 to become Thunder Bay. That same year, by a roundabout route, I arrived in Buffalo.

Everyone living in Thunder Bay knows about the grain elevators and I knew them particularly well. My father worked in the Manitoba Pool 1 elevator. Pool 1 sits in a row of elevators ranged along Lake Superior in the "intercity" area that lay between Fort William and Port Arthur. I later took my turn at elevator work, but it was an earlier job with the Canadian National Railway that provided my first real introduction to the elevators. Railroads and elevators go together. Grain comes into the elevators in Thunder Bay from western Canada in railway cars. When a grain car arrives in Thunder Bay, it has to be accounted for, sent to the right elevator and, once emptied, the car has to be returned to the train yard to be sent west to be loaded again.

My uncle Art worked as a brakeman on the CNR and, when he told me the railroad was looking for car checkers, I jumped at the chance to get the job. It was a very good summer job for a high school kid, but you had to be sixteen to work on the railroad. I was fifteen. I got the job, but I kept putting off bringing in my birth certificate. When I did deliver it the next summer, the yardmaster looked at it for a while and handed it back to me without saying anything. I took that as a successful review of my first summer's work.

A car checker keeps track of the railroad cars that sit in a switching yard. I started in the large CNR switching yard located in the intercity area not far from Manitoba Pool 1. In my first summer, I worked the midnight shift. At least once a night, I had to walk the length of all of the tracks in the yard. The tracks in a switching yard run off a "lead" track and the tracks get shorter as you move along the lead. The outside and longest track was always filled with empty boxcars waiting for their return trip west, and I had to take the long, dark walk beside it each working night. The light of the kerosene lantern I carried in the fold in my left arm would show a trail of grain along the ground beside the track. That loose grain had dropped from the empty boxcars as they were shunted in and out of the track. The kernels of grain looked more attractive to rats than to me. Every once in a while I'd hear scurrying in the dark and would be glad that I'd tied shoelaces tight around the bottom of my pant legs. I never really believed the stories that the switchmen told of rats running up your pant leg, but I didn't want to take the chance. They all go together: boxcars, elevators, grain, rats. And, yes, the fast-moving shadows under the boxcars were cats. But you wouldn't want to mess with them.

In the summer after my last year in high school, I was lucky to get a job at the Lakehead Planning Board. (Before Port Arthur and Fort William amalgamated, the two cities were collectively known as the "Lakehead.") That job ended my connection with car checking and the CNR, so, in the summer after my first year at university, I had to look farther for a job. I found one in a grain elevator. The Searle elevator was located outside Fort William near the mouth of the Kaministiquia River—known locally as the "Kam." Again, it was a good job that paid well and I didn't have to lie about my age to get it. Unfortunately, it didn't last long. I could put up with the noise of the elevator and I didn't mind the work. I could handle the job of shoveling up grain that had spilled from the conveyor belts and I could adjust the temperature in the dryers once I learned how to listen to instructions over the near-deafening noise of the drying machine, but I could not handle the dust.

Grain dust is everywhere in an elevator. It's a constant and unavoidable companion. For most, grain dust is annoying, causing red, itchy spots around the neck and elbows, but, for me, dust was a serious problem. I developed full-blown grain dermatitis. When I got home from work I filled a bathtub with cold water and lay in the tub until the itch I felt from head to foot went away. I thought I might get over it or that the problem would ease and I would learn to tolerate it, but the itch got worse. After two weeks, I told the elevator manager that I couldn't work in the elevator any longer; I collected a check for two weeks' pay and left.

Many years later, I arrived in Buffalo. By then, I had graduated from the University of Toronto and had a PhD in English from the University of Rochester. From Rochester, I joined the English faculty at the State University of New York at Buffalo. I lived and taught in Buffalo for fourteen years and remember being impressed by the many—then largely abandoned—elevators lining the Buffalo River. That impression, however, was peripheral. I saw the elevators on the Buffalo River out of the corner of my eye as I took my son fishing in a pond at the Tifft Farm Nature Preserve south of the city.

I have since opened my eyes and looked closely. I now see how important grain handling and elevators were and are to the city. The terminal grain elevator was invented in Buffalo and the city and the grain industry grew together. Elevators were central to Buffalo's history and their recognition and preservation has become important to many Buffalonians. That discovery led to others, some quite unexpected. For example, I learned that images of the grain elevators in Buffalo and Thunder Bay had inspired the development of European modernist architecture in the early twentieth century. It's not easy to combine the experience of working in an elevator with the idea of modernist architectural theory—especially for me. I can share the modernists' admiration for the monumentality of grain elevators, but I know something they probably didn't—that it's noisy, dusty, and dangerous to work in one.

I have returned to Thunder Bay to reconnect with the elevators there and I've traveled to Buffalo to talk to Buffalonians who know the history of the grain elevators in Buffalo and understand their value. The Thunder Bay elevators no longer handle the volume of grain they once did, but they still play a major role in the international grain trade. They are a striking presence in the city and dominate any postcard view of the Thunder Bay waterfront. In Buffalo, there are now only three working elevators. The grain that comes into Buffalo is, for the most part, used locally for feed or for making flour and breakfast cereal. While the Buffalo elevators no longer transfer millions of bushels of grain to other places in the United States and the world, some have taken on a new and different life. They are being incorporated into the cultural life of the city. Buildings that once housed grain now house art displays, musical performances, and theatrical spectaculars.

There is a lot to say about what grain elevators have meant, how they work, and what they may become. That's what this book is about.

Acknowledgments

I have received a great deal of help and encouragement in writing this book. My friend Judy Slater paved my path into the world of Buffalo elevators by introducing me to Beth Tauke. Beth's enthusiasm for Buffalo's Silo City elevators is contagious and has inspired many, including her students at SUNY Buffalo, School of Architecture and Planning. Many of her colleagues share her love of the Buffalo elevators, in particular, Kerry Traynor, who has secured a place for the American Grain Elevator Complex on the National Register of Historic Places.

Closer to home in Jamaica Plain, Massachusetts, I want to thank my neighbor, Jonathan McConathy, for his expert help with the illustrations in the book.

I have depended on others who have written about Buffalo and its elevators. Reyner Banham's *A Concrete Atlantis* (1986) is the classic book on the architecture of Buffalo elevators. It has inspired others to think and write about the subject, including William J. Brown in his book *American Colossus: The Grain Elevator, 1843 to 1943* (2009) and all of the contributors to *Reconsidering Concrete Atlantis: Buffalo Grain Elevators*, edited by Lynda H. Schneekloth (2006). Francis Kowsky has written about, and lectured on, the history of grain elevators in Buffalo. I thank "Frank" Kowsky, Lynda Schneekloth, Rick Smith, Jim Watkins, and all of the others who took time to talk to me about the Buffalo elevators. I should also acknowledge Timothy Bohen's book *Against the Grain* (2012) for teaching me about "scoopers" and the people of Buffalo's First Ward. Thanks also to the staff of the Buffalo History Museum for their help with my research there.

I grew up in Thunder Bay, Ontario, but I left many years ago and had to be reintroduced to the city's elevators. That reintroduction started with Joe Fiorito, a writer for the *Toronto Star*. I called him after reading his article in the *Star* about the Thunder Bay elevators and he referred me to Nancy Perozzo, the guiding spirit behind Thunder Bay's Friends of Grain Elevators. Nancy knew just what I should do and who I should talk to in Thunder Bay to explore the workings of the city's elevators.

The Friends of Grain Elevators and the Lakehead Social History Institute cooperated on an oral history project entitled The Voices of the Grain Trade. Bob Speak provided one of the narratives in that recorded collection and I have used Bob's account in my description in chapter 6 of the December 1952 explosion of Thunder Bay's Pool 4A. I am grateful to Ernie Epp, the co-director of the Lakehead Social History Institute, for permission to use the recording made by Bob Speak.

My knowledge of Thunder Bay expanded through my reading of Thomas W. Dunk's book, *It's A Working Man's Town* (1991), Thorold J. Tronrud and A. Ernest Epp's, *Thunder Bay, from Rivalry to Unity* (1995), and two books by Jean Morrison, *The North West Company in Rebellion* (1988) and *Labour Pains* (2009). I'm grateful that Gerry Heinrichs, Ryan Fay, Tom Hamilton, Herb Daniher, Cody Hubert, and others were willing to tell me, firsthand, about their experiences in the Thunder Bay elevators. I would also like to thank the director and staff of the Thunder Bay Museum. They provided access to the museum's files on elevator construction and operation and to accounts of local elevator disasters. The museum also provided important illustrations for this book.

I'm always grateful for the welcome I receive from my relatives in Thunder Bay, and I am particularly thankful for the support that Archie and Donna Otto gave to me while working on this book and for the help and encouragement of my uncle, Bill Beavis.

In Buffalo, the welcoming hospitality and practical assistance of Jerry and Judy Slater made working in Buffalo a pleasure.

There are at least two general debts that I owe. One is to Milo Smith Ketchum whose book on *The Design of Walls, Bins, and Grain Elevators*, first published in 1907 and revised in 1911, provided me with a thorough introduction to grain elevator construction (although I would have been better able to appreciate it if I had been trained as an engineer). The second is to Charles R. Morris. Charlie's book *The Dawn of Innovation* (2012) inspired me to think and write about shipping and industrial operations. It is the latest in a line of challenging and interesting books he has written on an amazing range of subjects.

Special thanks are due for the love and support of my wife, Carol Houlihan Flynn, and my children and stepchildren, Emily Siegel, Andrew Tarbet, Patrick Flynn, and Molly Morrissey.

1

Buffalo

Where Grain Elevators Were Born

All the waters of the upper Great Lakes push past Buffalo as they flow under the Peace Bridge and down the Niagara River to Lake Ontario. Looking at a map of North America, you might imagine that a ship launched on the north shore of Lake Superior could sail down the Great Lakes and on through the St. Lawrence River to the sea. That imagined trip can't happen. Roughly halfway down the Niagara River between Lake Erie and Lake Ontario is one immense, magnificent obstacle—Niagara Falls. As long as there was no way to avoid Niagara Falls, Buffalo held a key geographic advantage. From the west, it was the last stop before the Niagara River. From the east, it was the jumping-off place where settlers could sail west to Ohio and beyond. But that advantage wasn't fully realized until there was an easier way to travel between Buffalo and the East Coast. A water route from Buffalo to New York would provide that route, but it didn't appear until 1825.

On Wednesday, October 26, 1825, at ten o'clock in the morning, a cannon was fired in Buffalo. Its sound traveled east to start a string of cannon fire along the whole length of a newly built canal and, when it reached Albany, the cannon sound was carried on down the Hudson River to New York City. At twenty minutes past eleven o'clock that same morning, the cannon relay reached Fort Lafayette in New York harbor and a grand salute was fired. As the salute ended, the relay was repeated westward, up the Hudson River and along the new canal to Buffalo. The Erie Canal was officially open.

It had taken more than eight years of hard manual labor to dig the canal and create the bridges, aqueducts, and locks that made the 363-mile trip from Albany to Buffalo by water possible. Governor DeWitt Clinton had broken ground for the construction of the canal on July 4, 1817. Clinton had failed to get federal financing for the project but managed to obtain money for the seven million dollar cost of construction by issuing New York State–backed bonds. It was a bold and innovative move that proved a good gamble. The bonds were quickly repaid from tolls collected from canal travelers, and canal traffic grew to be greater than its planners ever expected.

The canal was dug from east to west and, as it approached Lake Erie, a fierce argument arose about its western terminus. Clinton wanted the canal to end in Buffalo, but he was maneuvered out of his seat on the Erie Canal Commission in April 1824 by his political opponents. For a time, it looked as if the promoters of Black Rock (a site north of Buffalo) would succeed in making that town the western end of the canal. There were good arguments for Black Rock. It had a better natural harbor than Buffalo and already handled more lake freight traffic. Buffalo, on the other hand, had no real harbor and its waterfront was exposed to dangerous waves from Lake Erie.

As the arguments went back and forth, Buffalo found itself playing defense. Both Buffalo and Black Rock had been burned to the ground by British troops in the War of 1812. Eleven years after the end of the war, memories of the conflict still lingered. That didn't help Black Rock, since its location on the Niagara River north of Buffalo exposed it to cannon fire from Fort Erie in Canada. That worry might have been set aside, but two other considerations finally tipped the balance in Buffalo's favor.

The first was the initiative taken by Buffalo merchants. In 1820, under the leadership of Samuel Wilkeson, Buffalo merchants had a channel dug out of the mouth of the Buffalo Creek and built a pier to protect the harbor that the channel created. (This protection was later supplemented by a series of breakwaters that created the Erie Basin Marina and expanded the city's harbor area.) The second factor was more technical and practical. Four of the five canal engineers who were in charge of the project wanted the canal to end at Buffalo. The water level was higher in Buffalo and more likely to feed the canal. Since Black Rock was slightly down the Niagara River from the lake, getting ships in and out of its harbor presented difficulties. After unloading, ships would have to work back into Lake Erie against the current of the river. And finally, Black Rock Harbor was vulnerable to damage from ice drifting in from Lake Erie. The last concern proved justified by extensive ice damage to Black Rock harbor in both 1824 and 1825.

Buffalo was finally chosen as the western terminus of the canal, and the canal engineers probably deserved credit for that decision. But the initiative of the Buffalo merchants is remembered as the reason for victory. Samuel Wilkeson is buried in Buffalo's Forest Lawn Cemetery along with other distinguished citizens of the city. The Latin inscription on his tombstone honors him for the creation of Buffalo's harbor and for guaranteeing Buffalo's growth into a thriving urban center. It reads: *Urbem Condidit*, "He Built the City."

DeWitt Clinton's fortunes revived after Buffalo's success. Indignation over his removal from the Erie Canal Commission was so great that the Peoples Party made him their candidate for governor of New York (his own party had not nominated him for reelection) and he again became governor in 1825. That gave him the opportunity to savor the completion of the canal he had envisioned and made possible. To attend the October 1825 opening of the Erie Canal in Buffalo, he and a large delegation traveled along the canal in the Seneca Chief all the way from Albany. After the opening ceremony in Buffalo, Clinton took the return trip down the canal and the Hudson River to New York City. When he got there, he poured two casks of Lake Erie water into the ocean water of New York harbor and set off another celebration. The *Niles Weekly Register* claimed that the celebration included banners, ornamentation, parties, and balls "the like of which never has before been witnessed in America."

The obvious symbolism of Clinton's celebratory trip was that the canal ran two ways. That two-way travel promoted enormous growth at both ends. Buffalo grew suddenly from a town of about 2,400 to a city of more than 42,000 by 1850. At the same time,

New York City grew to displace Philadelphia as the biggest shipping port on the Atlantic coast of the United States. Settlers could now move easily and cheaply from the East Coast to establish a new life in the western United States and, eventually, the products from their farms could find a convenient way to eastern markets.

In truth, the movement of farm products from the West developed slowly. The Erie Canal carried more people than goods in its earliest days. In 1828, the schooner *Guerriere* brought 2,500 bushels of wheat from the West, but there was no demand for it in Buffalo and it was not forwarded down the canal to New York but sent farther along the south shore of Lake Erie to Dunkirk. Part of the reason for the disappointing reception of the *Guerriere* was that moving grain from the lake to the canal wasn't easy. The original Erie Canal was forty feet wide and four feet deep. The largest boat able to manage in the canal could carry no more than thirty tons of grain. Wheat weighs about sixty pounds a bushel, so the *Guerriere*'s cargo would have filled two canal boats and half of another. It would also have to be moved from lake boat to canal boat manually, and that was hard work. Every bushel of bulk grain would have had to be drawn up from the cargo hold of the lake boat by block and tackle, one barrel at a time. It would then have to be weighed with a hopper and scales and either swung over the ship's side into the hatch of a canal boat or carried in baskets to a warehouse for later loading into a canal boat. This was the method employed for many years and, by this method, if the weather was good, a team of workers over a long, steady, and hard-working day could remove about eighteen hundred to two thousand bushels of grain from a lake boat. Unloading the *Guerriere* would have taken more than a day.

Despite these discouraging difficulties, it still made sense to move grain through Buffalo and down the Erie Canal to New York City and on to other eastern markets. The alternative was to send Western grain down one of the rivers that fed into the Mississippi and on down that river to New Orleans where it could be loaded on a ship for the voyage around Florida to markets on the East Coast. That trip took about three months and provided many opportunities for the grain to be lost or spoiled. It also carried a cost of about $100 a ton. Transportation costs for shipping via the Erie Canal were about $10 a ton and the grain would get to market more quickly with less chance of loss. Once the choice of the Erie Canal route through Buffalo was clear, the city began a steady climb toward grain shipping dominance.

By 1841, grain was arriving in Buffalo at the rate of two million bushels a year. Since, grain was still shifted by hand from lake boat to canal boat, demand for workers was high. Irish immigrants who arrived in the United Sates around this time were told that they could always find work in Buffalo. As long as this work was done manually, unloading for each boat was fixed at a top rate of eighteen hundred to two thousand bushels a day.

The lake ships now arriving in Buffalo were much bigger than the *Guerriere* and they lined up in Buffalo harbor waiting their turn to be unloaded. It seemed to Joseph Dart, a Buffalo merchant, that there must be a better way. The manual method of unloading grain, barrel by barrel, was too costly and too slow. What was needed, in Dart's opinion, was an effective and efficient mechanical method of removing the grain from a lake boat into a storage facility and out again into the canal boats.

Dart had been born in Connecticut and moved to Buffalo when he was twenty-two years old to become a retail merchant in the hat and fur business. He seems to have been, in every way, a practical and clear-headed man. It must have seemed strange, therefore, when this retail merchant began to puzzle over the delay suffered by the grain ships in Buffalo harbor or to imagine that he could find a mechanical way to move that grain. Mahlon Kingman, a forwarding merchant in Buffalo, had tried and failed to use an elevating device operated by horse power to remove grain from a lake boat into a building on the Evans Canal in Buffalo. He couldn't make it work. That prompted Dart to build a different device, but Kingman wasn't encouraging. He tapped Dart on the shoulder and said, "Dart, I am sorry for you; I have been through that mill; it won't do; remember what I say: Irishmen's backs are the cheapest elevators ever built."

What Kingman might not have known, and Dart did, was that the mechanics of elevating grain out of a ship into a building had already been conceived and accomplished. The third patent issued by the U.S. Patent Office was granted to Oliver Evans in December

1790. It was for an automated flourmill—a remarkable device able to process wheat delivered to a water-powered mill into flour automatically. First, wheat was dumped into a hopper; then, without any intervention from a worker, it was turned into flour that was bagged and ready to use. Evans's invention was so revolutionary that even when neighboring millers saw the mill in operation, they dismissed it as impossible and declared it "a set of rattle traps, not worth the notice of men of common sense." A few years later, when the device proved to be remarkably successful in the Ellicott mills of Baltimore, the same dismissive Brandywine millers of Delaware wanted to adopt the invention without paying Evans license fees and challenged his patent on the grounds that it was based on obvious and antique methods. Evans was able to defend his patent, but the cost and expense of litigation took a toll on the self-taught Delaware farm boy.

In 1792, Evans moved to Philadelphia where he published *The Young Mill-Wright and Miller's Guide* in 1795. By 1860, it had gone through fifteen editions. The book explained the principles and operation of his automated flourmill in detail. In one of the editions, he included a plate illustrating his mill. On the left hand side of the illustration, there is a ship docked next to the mill. The ship contains a load of grain, and an elevating device extends down into the ship. The device is an endless strap revolving around two pulleys. The bottom pulley is set in the grain that is to be hoisted into the mill from the hold of the ship. A series of buckets on the strap scoop up the grain and move it to the top where it is emptied into the mill as each bucket passes over the top pulley. Evans called this piece of his machine an "elevator" and the device in the illustration is a rudimentary version of what Dart would call a "marine leg." This elevator was the mechanical key to the fast and effective method of unloading grain that Dart was looking for and Dart, with the engineering help of Robert Dunbar, turned it into a commercial success. In doing so, the device that performed the elevating part of the process gave its name to the whole structure and operation, and the "elevator" was born.

Dart's elevator was finished in 1843. The elevator building was wooden and the elevator machinery was powered by a high-pressure steam engine of the sort that Oliver Evans had gone on to design later in his life. The elevator's storage bins held 55,000 bushels of grain, and the elevator was an immediate commercial success. Within three years, the capacity of the elevator had doubled, making Mahlon Kingman confess: "Dart, I find I did not know it all."

The schematic drawing in Fig. 1.1 shows the operation of Dart's elevator in simplified form.

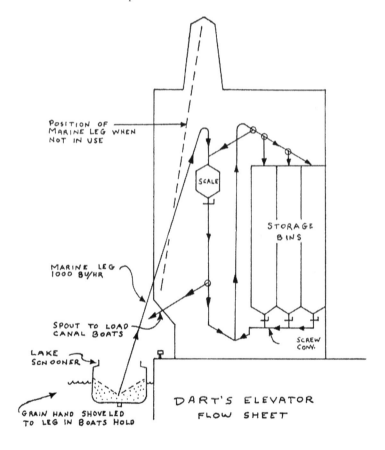

Figure 1.1. Schematic Drawing of Dart's Elevator. This drawing shows the operation of Dart's elevator, including two "legs." One is the labeled Marine Leg that lifts the grain out of a lake schooner. The other is an unlabeled leg that lifts the grain internally. A "leg" is another name for the belt and scoop lifting device that is basic to the workings of an elevator. This elevating device gives the "elevator" its name. Courtesy of Buffalo History Museum, used by permission.

Dart acknowledged his debt to Evans when he addressed the members of the Buffalo Historical Society on March 13, 1865. Evans, he said, deserves a place beside Robert Fulton and Eli Whitney as an inventive genius and benefactor of the commercial and industrial life of the United States. Later in the same speech, he called Evans "the Watt of America." By the time that Dart gave his address, there were twenty-nine working elevators in Buffalo, twenty-seven on land and two floating in the harbor. Together they could hold six million bushels of grain and were able to move in a day more grain than had come into Buffalo in the year that Dart built his elevator.

Dart wasn't as forthcoming in his credit to Robert Dunbar whose engineering skills and experience were essential to the building of Dart's elevator. That was probably the result of Dart's effort to obtain a patent for the invention of the grain elevator and his reluctance, therefore, to have Dunbar pictured as a participant in the invention. In the end, no patent was granted. Dart reaped the financial returns from the operation of his elevator, and Dunbar seemed satisfied to profit from designing elevators for others.

Perhaps Dart had worried too much about Dunbar. He seemed a man unlikely to challenge Dart or claim a part in his patent application. A contemporary described him as a man of "a singular retiring and undemonstrative disposition." Little is known of him beyond his having been born in Scotland in 1812 and having been trained as a mechanical engineer in Canada. After his engineering training, he moved to Buffalo in 1834. He would have been twenty-two years old—the same age that Dart was when he moved to the city. How Dart and Dunbar met is unknown, but somehow Dart had the sense to recognize Dunbar's engineering talent and to engage him in his elevator-building project. After playing a major role in the design and building of Dart's elevator, Dunbar went on to design most of the early elevators that were built in Buffalo. He became so well known as a grain elevator designer that he was sought out to design elevators and to supervise their construction far beyond Buffalo in Canada and Europe.

Whether Dart deserved a patent is still debated. He had found a different application for Evans's invention and turned what Evans had conceived as part of a manufacturing process into a process for the commercial transfer of grain. But since no patent was issued, the field was open to others to build grain elevators in the United States, Canada, and overseas without acknowledging or paying Dart. And build them they did.

In 1847, grain elevators were built in Toledo, Ohio, and Brooklyn, New York. Elevators in Toledo, Buffalo, and Brooklyn created a natural loop. Grain grown in Ohio traveled to Toledo to be processed and stored in the Toledo elevator. It was then loaded onto lake boats and shipped to Buffalo for transfer via the Buffalo elevators and the Erie Canal to New York City. The Brooklyn elevator received and stored grain for later distribution to East Coast flourmills and to grain consumers in England, the Netherlands, and Germany.

By 1900, a postcard picture of Buffalo harbor shows a busy grain trading port. Lake boats deliver their cargo of grain to the elevators, while tugboats pull barges loaded with grain up the Buffalo River on their way to the Erie Canal. Smokestacks rise above the plants that power the elevators, which are all built of wood in the style of Dart's original.

Figure 1.2. This photograph shows some of Buffalo's early wooden elevators. They stretch from the foot of Main Street along the Buffalo River. A lake boat is docked at the Eastern Elevator (the second on the left) and a tugboat in the foreground pulls a loaded canal barge along the river. The smokestacks beside the elevators show that they are steam powered. Courtesy of Library of Congress Prints and Photographs Division. LC-DIG-det-4a07180.

The successful operation of this Toledo-Buffalo-Brooklyn loop encouraged more and more settlers to establish themselves on farms in the West. This, consequently, led to the creation of similar loops that included more and more cities. Elevators appeared in Cleveland, Chicago, and Duluth as grain farming moved west. The same process worked in Canada, although Canadian shipping routes to the East were inserted in the Canadian loop. But a great deal of Canadian grain was shipped through Buffalo. It would be sent in bond though Buffalo and out of United States ports on the East Coast, thus avoiding custom duties that would otherwise have been levied on grain imported into the United States.

There was, of course, a natural limit to the westward extension of elevators in this grain-shipping loop. Lake Superior is the most westerly of the Great Lakes and, therefore, its north shore is as far west as a lake boat can reach. Duluth sits on the southwestern tip of the north shore of Lake Superior and Thunder Bay lies roughly on the lake's north shore mid-point. The establishment of elevators in those cities was inevitable. Both cities, therefore, became and remain major grain shipping ports. In their respective countries, they represent the farthest reach west of the commercial loop in grain shipments reaching eastern North American markets and beyond.

Buffalo, because of changes in shipping patterns, has seen its role in the grain shipping trade diminish. Grain production and shipping, however, continue. In order to follow the development of grain elevators it is necessary to move away from the story of the invention of terminal grain elevators to an account of their development and to what it takes to make them work.

2

⁓

Thunder Bay

Where Grain Dust Still Flies

Just west of Thunder Bay on Highway 17, there is a small sign marking the midpoint of Canada. The sign sits halfway between the farthest point in eastern Canada and the farthest point in western Canada. The fact that Thunder Bay is in the middle has been its fate and fortune. That, along with one other geographical blessing, makes the city important. Thunder Bay is not only in the middle of Canada, it sits on the north shore of Lake Superior at the top of the Great Lakes. That puts the city about as far west as you can go on the Great Lakes while still being in Canada.

When the North West Company had to look for an inland headquarters for its fur trading business, a location in the middle of the country with access to Lake Superior was ideal, and it chose Thunder Bay. Ever since, anyone wanting to move goods from western Canada (east of the Rocky Mountains) had to consider a route through Thunder Bay. If you could get goods to Thunder Bay, you could ship them on from there by water to eastern North America and to the parts of the world touched by the Atlantic Ocean.

The North West Company was one of two bitter rivals for dominance of the fur trade in Canada. Its better-known competitor was the Hudson Bay Company. The Hudson Bay Company held a monopoly on access to Hudson Bay. That focused the company's efforts on Hudson Bay in the north, where its trading posts radiated out from York Factory. The North West Company operated farther south and its trapping and trading business included southern Canada and extended into parts of what is now the United States south and west of the Great Lakes. In the far west, the North West Company also operated along the Columbia River in what is now Washington State.

Both the Hudson Bay Company and the North West Company were essentially British enterprises. For the North West Company, this meant that conducting its business in the parts of North America that would eventually become the United States proved to be more and more uncomfortable. Tensions grew between the United States and Britain before and after 1776, and those tensions led to clashes with American fur traders in areas claimed by the United States. In order to continue to conduct its fur trading business away from these dangers, the North West Company had to squeeze northward and run an all-Canadian business.

When the Jay Treaty made the Pigeon River part of the boundary between the United States and Canada in 1794, the North West Company's canoe route along the Pigeon to Grand Portage on Lake Superior became unworkable, since the end of that route had become part of the United States. The company had to look farther north for access to Lake Superior. If you move upward along the north shore of Lake Superior from Grand Portage, Minnesota, the Kaministiquia River is the next major river that flows into Lake Superior and provides a possible connection with the west. The North West Company decided to build a wooden stockade fort near the mouth of the Kaministiquia River in 1803 and to use it as a transfer point in moving furs from western Canada to its headquarters in Montreal. In 1807, the fort was named Fort William after William McGillivray, the chief partner of the North West Company. By 1815, Fort William had become the greatest fur trading post in the world.

The North West Company's logic in locating its inland head-quarters in Fort William was simple. Since it could no longer operate in United States territory, the company's transportation routes had to change. Its furs now came from the Athabasca Country—a vast area of northern Saskatchewan and Alberta. The company's business headquarters were in Montreal and the market for its furs was in London and continental Europe. It is a long way from the Athabasca Country to Montreal, so long in fact, that it was impossible to make a round trip by canoe from the Athabasca Country to Montreal and back during a single "season"—that time each year when the rivers and lakes are free of ice. This meant that the trip had to be divided into two parts. Canoes from the West had to meet and transfer their furs to canoes from Montreal at a central rendezvous point. With the Pigeon River closed to the North West Company, the rendezvous point became Fort William. Small trapper canoes could travel from the West to Fort William through lakes and rivers that only small canoes could manage. Large, "voyageur" canoes traveled up the St. Lawrence and through the Great Lakes all the way to Fort William. The exchange of furs from the trappers' to the voyageurs' canoes and the transaction of company business would take place in the fort over a roughly two-week period in mid-July. The paddlers would then leave the "Rendezvous" party. Some would head back west to Athabasca and the others would travel east to Montreal.

The pattern established by the fur trade cast Thunder Bay in the part it was destined to play. From its mid-country perspective, the major markets were east but, if goods had to get to those markets from the west, Thunder Bay offered the Canadian route.

After 1821, the flow of furs through Thunder Bay dwindled. Relentless pressure from the Hudson Bay Company on the North West Company eventually forced the North West Company into a merger with its rival. Business at Fort William slowed as the merged company sent most furs to Europe through Hudson Bay. The Hudson Bay Company maintained the fort, however, and kept some furs moving though it for many years.

Although Thunder Bay's location on the Canadian trade route had been established, it took a while before other products began to move through Thunder Bay. The forests around Thunder Bay were logged for lumber used for buildings in eastern Canada. Pulp logs from those same forests were turned into newsprint sent to the presses of the big cities of the East. Iron ore arrived from Atikokan for shipment to the steel mills in Hamilton and the United States. But preeminently, and above all else, Thunder Bay began to receive grain coming from the Prairie Provinces of Manitoba, Saskatchewan, and Alberta. Once the grain began to arrive, terminal elevators had to be built to handle it. The Thunder Bay elevators cleaned, dried, and sorted that grain before sending it to flour mills in southern Ontario, bakeries in Britain, and pasta factories in Italy, as they still do. Grain handling became a major Thunder Bay industry and, during the twentieth century, Thunder Bay succeeded for a time to the title once held by Buffalo as the busiest grain shipping port in the world.

Visitors to Thunder Bay can see a restored Fort William in operation, complete with a "Rendezvous" party in July. (The fort has been rebuilt on the Kam, but farther up the river, away from its original location.) While tourists can join in the Rendezvous party, there is another ceremony that no tourists ever get to witness. It harks back to fur trading days, but it also connects to modern grain handling in Thunder Bay. Every year, the captain of the first ship to arrive in the port of Thunder Bay after the winter ice has cleared receives a top hat. The hat is made, like all properly made top hats, from beaver fur—the most prized fur of all those handled by the North West Company.

The captain who receives that hat is almost always the captain of a lake boat arriving at one of the Thunder Bay elevators for a load of grain. In 2013, for example, the top hat went to Captain Douglas Parsons who sailed into Thunder Bay on the *John B. Aird* and docked at the Viterra elevator (formerly Saskatchewan Pool 7) on March 26. The local paper carried a picture of the top-hatted captain so that everyone in Thunder Bay knew the grain shipping season was open. What they likely did not know was the connection between the ceremonial top hat and the once-flourishing fur trading business of Fort William. It's a connection worth remembering. First furs then grain—these different products moved through Thunder Bay because of the same transportation imperatives.

But Thunder Bay's entry into the grain handling business depended on more than location. It also needed railways. Without railways to move grain from the West to Thunder Bay, its location meant little to western farmers. Right from the beginning, railroads and elevators were intimately related. At the same time that the Canadian Pacific Railway connected the Canadian prairies with Thunder Bay, it built an elevator in Port Arthur. That elevator, completed in 1883, was leased to Mr. King in 1891 and, consequently, became known as "King's" elevator. The elevator held 350,000 bushels of grain and was made of wood. It looked very much like Dart's elevator in Buffalo. Not long afterward, four other CPR elevators were built on the north bank of the Kaministiquia River in Fort William. Elevator A was wooden and was built in 1885. Elevator B was made of tile in 1889. Elevator C was also wooden and was built in 1890. Elevator D had steel tanks and was finished in 1902. Taken together, they could hold almost four million bushels of grain.

Other elevators were built at a steady pace. The Canadian Northern Railway followed the CPR in creating a railroad line linking Thunder Bay to the West and, once the link was made, built two elevators in Port Arthur in 1902. Its Elevator A was wooden and held one million bushels, but it also had tile storage tanks that held millions more. The Canadian Northern's wooden Elevator B also held a million bushels of grain.

In the midst of this elevator-building boom, my grandparents, along with many other immigrants, came to Thunder Bay. My Scottish grandparents arrived from Dundee in 1910 and my English grandparent arrived from the East End of London in 1912. Neither couple was drawn to the wooden sidewalks that covered the muddy streets of Thunder Bay by the elevators. My English grandfather was a carpenter and my Scottish grandfather had worked on the railroad in Dundee but decided to bring his salesman's charm to the new world. They knew only that Thunder Bay was growing and that it offered more chances for work and family than Britain provided.

They arrived before Europe plunged into World War I so that, without design, they avoided some of the pain caused by that war. It's not that Canada escaped the effects of the war. 620,000 Canadians joined the armed forces during the war and 66,000 died on the battlefields of Belgium and France. But despite, and because of, their sacrifice, Canada continued to grow. By the end of the war, eighteen more elevators augmented those I've already mentioned.

By 1939, Thunder Bay had the world's largest grain storage capacity—almost 93 million bushels. By 1964, there were twenty-eight active terminal elevators in Thunder Bay shipping an average of 300 million bushels of grain a year. In the following decade, grain shipping from Thunder Bay hit its high water mark. After that, shipments still remained strong, but changing markets and methods have taken a toll on the Thunder Bay elevators and today there are only seven active terminal grain elevators in Thunder Bay. Strangely, although there are fewer elevators, each one of them can handle more grain per elevator than ever before. The grain dust still flies in Thunder Bay. Almost six and a half million metric tons of grain was shipped in 2012. That is more than 238,000,000 bushels.

3

First Impressions

I first encountered grain elevators in Thunder Bay. I don't remember my exact age, but I was young and my father drove to the elevator. It couldn't have been a regular workday because he would have been out of the house before I woke up on working mornings. Perhaps he went in on a day off to get something he'd forgotten. He worked in Manitoba Pool 1, and you had to cross a bridge over the CNR switch yards at intercity to get to it. Once over the bridge, you could see a line of elevators stretching along the road, one after another, each standing large and monumental, pushing up against the edge of the lake. Pool 1 was near the end of the line. My father parked next to the elevator. When I got out of the car, the bins towered above me, big and white. A distant hum came from the dust extractors at the top of the bins and drifts of yellow dust hung in the air.

Elevators make you feel small. The bins may only be ten or twelve stories high, but they stretch upward without interruption in dominating concrete columns that make them appear much taller than other buildings of the same height. As we walked toward the open door of the elevator, I noticed the feral cats crouching in the grass that grew from kernels that had spilled from the boxcars that had been emptied in the car shed. Once inside, my impression of the elevator changed. What had seemed overwhelming from outside, altered and became mysterious. The massive bins could no longer be seen but they were felt. You knew that they stretched away in long rows one after the other five, six or seven ranks wide and you knew that all the grain they contained had a meaning and purpose beyond Thunder Bay. The millions of bushels of grain that surrounded you were there only for a short stay. The elevator sat beside Lake Superior, after all, so that lake boats and ocean ships could dock and take the grain away. The elevator wasn't built to hold grain, but to send it on.

It's impossible that I understood it at the time, but that sense of transience has stuck with me. I might have sensed that, like the grain, I too would eventually have to move on.

It is important to know that the Thunder Bay elevators, like the elevators in Buffalo, are "terminal" elevators. They are not places where grain is meant to be collected and stored. They were and are designed and built to move grain, not to hold it. They receive, treat, and ship large amounts of grain to the places where it will be used.

The terminal elevators of Buffalo and Thunder Bay are very different from the traditional elevators that were once spaced out along the railroad tracks across the American heartland and the Canadian Prairies. Those small, wooden elevators were collection points where the farmers who grew grain could deliver their crops. Those elevators were known as "primary" or "country" elevators. The grain they received would be sent on by rail to the terminal elevators in port cities or to other distribution centers. There were many of them when farmers brought their grain to a country elevator by horse and cart. When that was the only way that farmers could move their grain to market, there were thousands of them. There had to be so many in order to be within easy reach of the farms that supplied them.

There are far fewer now. Grain that once had to move by horse and cart can now be trucked to larger elevators located in strategic inland places. Some inland elevators are as big or bigger than terminal elevators and do many of the jobs, such as cleaning, drying, and grading grain, that the terminal elevators do. But these inland elevators are located far from shipping ports. The grain they hold still has to be sent on to terminal elevators in order to reach its final destination.

Primary or country elevators do, however, share something with the early elevator that Dart built in Buffalo—their looks. Dart's elevator functioned like a terminal elevator but it looked like a larger version of a country elevator. Dart built an elevator that resembled an overgrown wooden barn with a few extra parts. Frank Kowsky, a Buffalo historian, described the early Buffalo elevators as resembling "ungainly" sheds. They were topped with sloping roofs that protected their open-topped bins from the weather. To eyes that had been conditioned by elegant city buildings, Dart's elevator had a "country" feel and seemed out of place in an urban landscape. When the British novelist Anthony Trollope visited Buffalo in 1861 and recorded his impressions of the elevators that lined the Buffalo waterfront, each seemed to him, "As ugly a monster as has yet been produced." He admired the work they performed, but he didn't care for their looks.

That "country" look, however, has its admirers, and the small primary elevators with their wooden sides and slant-roof cupolas now have a devoted following. They are documented fondly and nostalgically as "Prairie Sentinels" in many photographic collections and paintings. In the meantime, terminal elevators moved on to a different and distinctive look. Dart's elevator and country elevators were and are made of wood. Wooden elevators located near railroads at a time when steam engines sent sparks from their smokestacks were vulnerable to fire.

There was more than one reason for this. The railroad steam engines were a threat and supplied the spark, but wooden elevators contained grain, which made them much more likely to burn. Grain is dusty and grain dust ignites easily. Once ignited, if it is in a confined space it explodes, and even if the fire wasn't spread through an explosion, the tops of the bins in early elevators were open and fire spread easily from one bin to another.

By the time that Dart addressed the Buffalo Historical Society in 1865, thirteen of the Buffalo elevators had burned and only eight of those that had burned were rebuilt. The loss of thirteen of twenty-nine elevators in the span of twenty-two years was a rate of destruction that could not be tolerated. New methods and materials had to be found that would make elevators more resistant to fire. In the process, modern terminal elevators emerged looking the way they look today.

In Buffalo, the transformation began in 1887 when the Great Northern Elevator was built. Its bins were made of steel and promised fire resistance. The steel bins were round and would have looked from the outside like the concrete elevators that are familiar today, but, for some reason, the structure was enclosed in a flat, brick curtain wall and had a gallery along the top with a pitched roof that was reminiscent of the older wooden elevators. That pitched roof didn't make much of an impression sitting on top of bins that would have towered over the wooden bins of Dart's elevator. The thirty biggest bins in the Great Northern Elevator were thirty-eight feet in diameter and stood eighty-five feet high. Each held 74,000 bushels of grain. The bins in Dart's elevator held about five thousand bushels.

The Great Northern's pitched-roof shed running along its top seemed added to maintain a stylistic connection to earlier elevators. When the Electric Elevator was built farther up the Buffalo River, it had no lingering stylistic elements from earlier elevators. It exposed its round steel bins proudly. But even steel had its problems. It was expensive and tended to rust. When exposed to fire, the steel bins heated and got so hot that the grain inside was roasted.

Other materials were tried. Elevator bins built of brick or from tile worked well, but building an elevator with these materials required highly skilled workers and took a long time. The material that eventually triumphed and, in North America at least, became the standard construction material for elevators, was reinforced concrete. It was strong enough to resist the pressure of the grain contained in the bins and benefited from the discovery of a remarkable construction method that allowed elevators to be built with a speed and ease never seen before.

Milo Smith Ketchum published the definitive guide to elevator construction, in 1907. It was appropriately called *The Design of Walls, Bins, and Grain Elevators* and, when it first appeared, it went systematically through the various materials that could be used to build elevator bins, starting with timber and going on through steel, concrete, tile, and brick. By the time it was republished in 1911, Ketchum had to admit that the choice had narrowed. He ended his chapter on the types of grain elevators with the admission that "the use of reinforced concrete for grain elevators has increased and the methods of construction have been improved, so that the present cost of reinforced concrete bins is generally less . . . [and it] has also been proved by experience with disastrous fires that reinforced concrete bins are more nearly fireproof than any other type of bin." Reinforced concrete had triumphed and that material dominated the great era of elevator building in North America in the early decades of the twentieth century.

Reinforced concrete succeeded as the material of choice because of an engineering marvel called "slip-form" construction. This construction method revolutionized the building of terminal elevators. The early master of the method was the Barrett & Record Company of Minneapolis, and the engineer in charge was William R. Sinks. Sinks was always careful to say that he didn't build the first concrete elevator. C. F. Haglin built it for the Peavey Company in Duluth, Minnesota.

Unfortunately, the first concrete elevator revealed some problems. Building was slow because the concrete was allowed to harden in the forms overnight before the forms were removed and placed on top of the hardened circle of concrete below. This building method made it difficult to keep each layer in line. The misalignment produced unsightly lines between the layers and, more importantly, created weaknesses. When the bins were finished and filled with grain, one of the bin walls gave way. This may also have had something to do with foreign materials contained in the sand and stone that were mixed into the concrete, but, whatever the cause, grain burst through the bin and showered onto the ground.

When William Sinks was approached by E. H. McHenry, the chief engineer of the Canadian Pacific Railway, with the idea of building a concrete elevator in Port Arthur, he wasn't keen. Sinks made sure that the quote for the concrete version was higher than his quote for a tile-binned elevator. He hoped this would ensure the choice of tile as the building material and relieve Barrett & Record of stress, since they knew how to build tile elevators successfully. But McHenry wanted concrete and opted for the high-priced model. He even contributed a key suggestion to Sinks. McHenry had traveled in Europe and seen a concrete culvert being built with moveable forms. As the concrete was being poured, the forms were moved forward. McHenry suggested that what could be done horizontally could also be done vertically. Sinks adopted the idea and the CPR elevator in Port Arthur was built with forms that could be jacked up vertically as concrete was poured into them. The method worked, and the CPR elevator was finished in 1905. A year later, the James Stewart Company designed the American Malting Company elevator in Buffalo—the first elevator in the United States built with reinforced concrete using the continuous-pour, slip-form construction method.

The apotheosis of concrete elevator building, however, was the Grand Trunk Pacific Elevator in Thunder Bay. The ambition and scope of plans for building that elevator were breathtaking. Behind it all was an international scheme of investment and enterprise. The Grand Trunk Railway operated out of Montreal and was financed from London. It already ran railroads in the United States stretching from Portland, Maine, to Chicago. Its next step was to build and run a railroad that would cross Canada from the Maritime Provinces to British Columbia. This goal was to be accomplished by creating a network of railways. The first part of the network consisted of the Grand Trunk Pacific Railway, running from Winnipeg, Manitoba, to the Pacific coast at Port Rupert, British Columbia. The National Transcontinental Railway would then run east from Winnipeg all the way to Moncton, New Brunswick. A spur line would link Thunder Bay with the network via a 190-mile track that joined the National Transcontinental Railway at Sioux Lookout, north and west of Thunder Bay.

On September 12, 1905, Prime Minister Sir Wilfred Laurier journeyed to Thunder Bay to turn the first sod for the construction of that spur line. With the prospect of a second railway link to Prairie grain, plans for a truly grand Thunder Bay elevator emerged. The Grand Trunk Pacific Railway acquired seven and a half square miles of land on the south bank of the Kaministiquia River across from

Mission Island near the mouth of the river. Plans were developed to build an elevator that would hold forty million bushels of grain—a capacity far beyond anything ever planned or built. The elevator was to be constructed in four separate sections with each of the sections holding ten million bushels of grain. Even one section would have surpassed any other Thunder Bay elevator, the biggest of which held less than seven million bushels. If it had been built as planned, it would have been an elevator with twice the capacity of the elevator that is today said to be the world's biggest, the DeBruce elevator in Hutchinson, Kansas. The DeBruce can hold almost twenty million bushels of grain.

In November 1908, Mayor James Murphy of Fort William traveled by boat to the site of the future Grand Trunk Pacific Elevator and led the celebration marking the beginning of the elevator's construction. Construction wasn't easy. Because of the low-lying ground on which the elevator was to be built, twelve hundred fifty-foot-long piles had to be driven into the ground to support the concrete platform on which the bins would rise. Worker had to deal with temperatures as low as 55 degrees below zero (Fahrenheit). Sometimes, materials needed for building froze solid.

Despite the difficulties, the carefully documented construction process proceeded. William Sinks was again called upon to supervise the process. Circular forms were built and a newly designed set of jacks used to raise the forms were installed. The new jacks operated more smoothly than those previously used and made the concrete surface of the bins seamless. By 1910, the Grand Trunk Pacific Elevator received its first shipment of grain, and by 1912, the first phase of building was complete. It was a fine elevator—an example of slip-form concrete construction at its best—but it hadn't matched the scale first planned. Its capacity was 5,700,000 bushels, less than 15 percent of what was initially projected. Still, it was and is a monument to elevator building and it became a fully realized model for all elevators in the future.

The March 1920 issue of *Successful Methods* magazine praised W. R. Sinks as the "Father of the Modern Concrete Elevator" and acknowledged that his slip-form method was now used to build all elevators.

The same article concluded that in the "years since, concrete elevators have gone up wherever there was grain to put in them . . . and to the eye the walls [are] as smooth as a cathedral column."

Other admiring eyes had also been cast on elevators. Modernist architects in Germany were captivated by them. They saw terminal elevators as the embodiment of pure form and put them on a level with the monuments of ancient Egyptians. They didn't like cathedrals, but pyramids were worthy of praise, and that praise was lavished on grain elevators. Wilhelm Worringer used the pyramid comparison in his 1908 book *Abstraction and Empathy*. Soon after, Walter Gropius remarked that American industrial buildings, particularly elevators, united symbol and structure in the same way they were united in the pyramids of Egypt.

Figure 3.1. The Grand Trunk Pacific Elevator, circa 1910. This photograph shows the Grand Trunk Pacific Elevator shortly after completion of construction. This was one of the elevators used as a model by modernist architects. Courtesy of the Thunder Bay Museum.

To make his point, Gropius included in his 1913 publication *The Development of Modern Industrial Building* seven pages of illustrations showing grain elevators. The illustrations included pictures of the Washburn-Crosby Elevator complex and the Dakota Elevator in Buffalo and of the Grand Trunk Pacific Elevator in Thunder Bay. The Washburn-Crosby was a tile and reinforced concrete elevator built between 1903 and 1909. The Dakota was a steel elevator built in 1901. The Grand Trunk Pacific Elevator was a particularly inspired choice since it represented the finished form of the modern concrete elevator and the model of all elevators to come.

How could elevators that once had seemed ungainly and ugly to sophisticated European travelers such as Anthony Trollope be so admired by later European architects? They were, of course, looking at very different things. The early elevators that Trollope saw in Buffalo could not survive. Their combustibility forced changes, and the new building materials used to protect the grain against fire changed the way elevators looked. The circular steel, brick, or tile bins appeared in proud rows as later elevators were built. The cathedral-like smooth, round bins of the reinforced concrete elevators succeeded them and became the prototype for all terminal elevators. Their bins stretched out in lines that were hundreds of feet long and stood side by side many ranks wide. The sloped roof that had covered the tops of early wooden elevators was replaced on later terminal elevators with a long, flat-roofed structure. This structure accommodated one or more conveyor belts running the full length of the elevator bins.

There was another very different element added to the modern elevator. This new element was the "workhouse" and it contrasted with the smooth circularity of the bins. It was a tall, rectangular structure with windows marking out its floors. Those floors held the machinery that made the elevator work and, in order for that machinery to be effective, the workhouse had to reach up higher than the top of the elevator bins. Bins are typically about 120 feet high, while workhouses can rise to 180 feet. The workhouse needed to be rise above the bins because it contained the garners and scales that received and weighed the grain that would eventually travel down into the bins. The workhouse also contains all of the machinery that powered the legs that lifted the grain and made the conveyor belts run.

The workhouse was either in the middle or at the end of most elevators and the combination of the monumental bins with the massive and powerful workhouse created the elevators that the modernists admired. When modernist architects looked at a grain elevator, they saw a building whose form was perfectly suited to what they thought of as its function.

It is important to remember that modernist architects related to grain elevators through their looks. Their knowledge of these buildings came from photographs. In the photos, they saw large, impressive structures with simple elements that were made of a material they loved—concrete. They knew little about how grain elevators worked or what it was like to work in them. The dust, the noise, the heat and cold that were everyday experiences for those working in grain elevators were not their concern. They saw the

Figure 3.2. "Elevator Alley" Buffalo. Patricia Bazelon's photograph reveals the majesty and beauty of the unused Buffalo elevators. Copyright 1987 Patricia Layman Bazelon. Used by permission of Lauren Tent.

GRAIN TERMINALS AT PT ARTHUR- FT WILLIAM. ONT-CANADA

Figure 3.3. A View of the Elevators on the Thunder Bay Waterfront. This photograph shows some of the many working elevators along Thunder Bay's Lake Superior waterfront. The view is to the north looking over the line of intercity elevators toward the Current River elevators in the distance. Courtesy of the Thunder Bay Museum.

stately workhouses rising above the height of the bins, but they didn't know anything about the machinery in those workhouses. Their interpretation of Gropius's illustrations was based on photographic impressions made by the exterior of the elevator buildings: massed rows of bins topped by a commanding workhouse. The functioning of the elevators was largely imagined. When I met with Lynda Schneekloth in Spot Coffee in downtown Buffalo, one of the first questions I asked her was how modernist architects such as Gropius, Erich Mendelsohn, and Le Corbusier could use elevators as a model for the whole modernist architecture movement when they seemed so removed from the reality of them? Besides, elevators weren't architectural creations. They were designed and built by engineers who thought more about how they worked than how they looked. I imagined that she was the right person to answer these questions since she had been a professor in the School of Architecture and Planning at the University of Buffalo and worked hard on efforts to preserve and reuse the Buffalo elevators.

We agreed that grain elevators have an impressive, monumental appearance and have a strong effect on anyone seeing them close up. We both knew that the ten or twelve story height of elevator bins was more overwhelming than a much higher building interrupted by windows like those that mark office or residential floors. But the link of modernism to elevators through photographs was more remote.

Her answer to the question of the modernists' love of elevators went beyond either the elevators' photographic attractiveness or their immediate impression. In her opinion, modernists of all stripes were ready to "throw everything out." The impulse wasn't exclusive to architects but was shared by many other thinkers in the early twentieth century. New materials such as steel and reinforced concrete meant that buildings could be made differently and that you didn't need the "old stuff" like the decorative details that had cluttered traditional buildings. Also, architects became more inclusive and less disdainful of other professions. Engineers were recognized as supplying many of the new ideas, materials, and designs that architects were looking for. Engineers appreciated the flexibility of new standardized materials and didn't mind when they were put together in ways that "didn't hide the joints."

If you imagine these ideas in the heads of architectural theorists, it is easier to understand how images of large, unadorned, engineer-designed buildings like elevators would appeal to them. Beyond all that, Lynda admitted that "there is an inherent beauty in something seeming to be exactly what it needs to be." If you have to store large amounts of grain, rows of concrete bins showing only the slightest impression of the forms that have been hoisted up to create them can look both tough and beautiful. Taken together, these ideas explain how the cluster of elevators along the Buffalo River or the stretch of elevators along the lakefront in Thunder Bay could be seen as impressive monuments to the power and beauty of modern industrialism.

4

Managing an Elevator

It wasn't easy getting to the Richardson elevator on April 19, 2013. The snow in Thunder Bay had started the night before and by morning it was still falling and the wind was blowing—hard. The van struggled out of the street where I was staying, but the main roads weren't bad. The snow got deeper when I turned off North Cumberland Street and took the overpass toward the elevator. Down the road, the tall white bins of the Richardson elevator could barely be seen through the blowing snow and I wondered about getting back through the drifts that were building across the road.

The security guard in the visitors shed at the end of the parking lot looked surprised to see me. "Write in any leaving time you want right now; I won't be here when you get back," he said. After I'd signed the visitor book, I walked toward the loading dock, if you can call sliding one foot carefully ahead of the other walking. The wind, already strong, doubled as it hit and deflected down the bins of the elevator. It tried to push me across the loading dock toward the ice floating in the slip that opened into Lake Superior. The water looked cold and dangerous.

The door leading to the elevator offices was half way down the loading dock. I took my time getting there, reaching my left hand out for the bin wall all the way along. Gerry Heinrichs looked a little surprised when I walked into his office. I was expected, but, given the weather, I might not have arrived on time. The elevator had been scheduled for a busy day. A lake ship was supposed to be loaded, but the strong wind had prevented its maneuvering into the slip. Rail cars had also been expected, but even the railroad couldn't make it through the snow and the wind. All in all, it was the perfect day for my interview. There weren't likely to be any interruptions.

Gerry looked relaxed and easygoing as he sat behind his desk. As I fiddled with the recorder, he joked that this could be a difficult interview because, "English was not [his] mother tongue." I thought he was making excuses for his prairie accent, but that wasn't it. He was born in Lowe Farm, Manitoba, a community of German speakers who had immigrated to Canada for religious reasons. He spoke German until he went to school at six and had to learn English. Some odd effects still lingered. He sometime asked people for their "front name," transposing the German word for "first name." But the school did a good job. His English is prairie perfect.

It seemed to me that he had come a long way from a remote farm town well south of Winnipeg and well north of Grand Forks, North Dakota. The obvious question was how he got to be in the job of regional manager of the Richardson elevator in Thunder Bay, Ontario? The answer was easy: he asked. Gerry grew up farming but left the farm to train as a meat cutter. He soon found that he didn't like meat cutting, so, at twenty, he applied for the job of manager of the Pioneer elevator in Morden, Manitoba. He got the job on the spot. In fact, they wanted him to start that day.

In Gerry's mind, the offer created two problems. He needed to give notice at the job he had. The second problem was more serious. He knew nothing about managing a prairie elevator. Pioneer didn't think either problem that difficult. They would give him time to provide notice and assured him that someone would be at the elevator to show him the ropes. Two months later, he watched apprehensively out the elevator office window as the fellow he had been working with and who had taught him the little he then knew about the elevator business drove away. But there was a realization that went beyond the apprehension. The elevator might be small, but he was the boss at twenty-one years of age and he hadn't even gone to university. That kind of opportunity looks remarkable today.

The company Gerry started with, Pioneer Grain Company, is a subsidiary of James Richardson International Limited. Richardson is a large, diversified company founded by an Irish immigrant to Canada, James Richardson, in 1857. James Richardson worked as a tailor in Kingston, Ontario. He expected to get most of his work from the military by making uniforms for the soldiers and sailors based there, but he found that local residents also wanted tailoring services. Since the locals were farmers, they found it more convenient to pay James in grain. Cash was often scarce.

When James, in turn, had to arrange for the sale of the grain, he found that trading grain was more profitable than tailoring. There was a market for grain in the United States, and he soon had ships carrying grain across the eastern end of Lake Ontario to New York ports. That led James Richardson to found a company to conduct his grain handling business and the company built an elevator in Kingston. Shortly afterward, his company built another elevator at Neepawa, Manitoba, in the grain-rich Canadian Prairies. The company's business developed quickly. Business expanded to such an extent that the Richardson Company was the first Canadian grain handling company to ship wheat from Western Canada through the Canadian lake system to Liverpool, England. That was in 1883.

Like many other large grain handling companies, the Richardson Company is essentially a family business that has always been headed by a Richardson. Now its interests extend far beyond grain. The company is involved in finance, real estate, manufacturing, transportation, and oil and gas development. But it began as, and it remains, a grain company and it now owns many elevators. Some, like the one Gerry managed in Morden, Manitoba, were "primary" or "country" elevators—wooden elevators that were once strung out across the Canadian Prairies from Manitoba through Alberta. Few of these elevators remain. At present, most Richardson elevators are large inland and terminal elevators. They can handle millions of bushels of grain.

Terminal elevators are in major shipping ports such as Thunder Bay at the head of the Great Lakes, or Churchill on Hudson Bay, or

Vancouver and Prince Rupert on the West Coast of Canada. Large, modern inland elevators that collect grain transported to them by farmers can now be even larger than terminal elevators. In fact, the largest elevator in the world is far from any shipping port, in the middle of Kansas. It is in Hutchinson, Kansas. That elevator is almost a half-mile long, and it holds 18.2 million bushels of grain. Its twenty-three-story-high reinforced concrete bins evoke wonder, not the nostalgia now often felt for the old wooden country elevators.

Gerry's career with Pioneer/Richardson took him back and forth over the prairie provinces of Manitoba and Saskatchewan. He managed individual elevators, regional groups of elevators, and, finally, oversaw all of Pioneer's grain handling operations. But his progress through the Richardson system wasn't without its bumps. After a few years managing Pioneer facilities in Bethune, Saskatchewan, he thought about quitting to attend the University of Manitoba. But at the company's suggestion, he took a drive along the beautiful Carrot River in Saskatchewan and liked what he saw. He liked it so much that he accepted the job Pioneer offered him to supervise the operations of its two elevators in the town of Carrot River. Carrot River was then one of the largest grain delivery points in the Prairies.

When, years later, he took over all of Pioneer's operations, he had to move to Richardson's head office in Winnipeg. The problem was, he didn't take to corporate life and chose to go back to hands-on work. Still, headquarters life had an effect on him. He now could think on a company-wide scale. While managing Richardson's operations near Regina, he got involved in health and safety issues and made it clear that he didn't like the way they were being handled in some of the other Richardson elevators. His bluff was called and he was told that, if he wanted to do anything about it, he would have to go back to where he didn't want to go—the Winnipeg head office. He went and managed the Environment, Health, and Safety department, but he still wasn't comfortable. One of the senior Richardson executives noticed his unhappiness and sat him down. He didn't mince words. "You don't like it here very much do you, boy? You need to get back into the field somewhere."

Getting back into the field meant a move to Ontario—first to southern Ontario, and finally to Thunder Bay, where he has managed the Richardson elevator for the last eight years—the longest he has ever stayed in any of his Richardson jobs. When Gerry first looked at Thunder Bay in 2005, he wasn't encouraged. It seemed to be in a depression. The sawmills were closing, paper mills were shutting down and the boom time for the Thunder Bay elevators had passed. But there were interesting challenges. It would be the first time he would manage a unionized work force and the Richardson elevator needed to be brought into the Richardson group. It had been separately organized and carried on largely as if it were independent. Besides, his wife loved Thunder Bay and Gerry felt that, if she wanted to settle in Thunder Bay, she deserved her chance after so many uncomplaining moves in the past.

But Gerry is still a little restless. If his wife were willing, he says, he would move on to another Richardson job "in a heartbeat." But that move may not be the most likely one. He respects his wife's wishes to stay in Thunder Bay—for now—but the next move could be entirely different. Gerry is in the process of donating a kidney to his brother-in-law. He reports that that same brother-in-law has always said that, when he—that's Gerry—grows up, "him and I are going to farm together." His brother-in-law already has the land, and Gerry would be happy to go back to farming—as long as he can go someplace warm in the winter.

You don't get the sense, however, that Gerry is unhappy in his job. Relations with the unions are good and the elevator now runs as an integral part of the Richardson grain business. In the end, running it is certainly an important job. At the time of our interview, the Viterra elevator, formerly Saskatchewan Pool 7, was the biggest local elevator, but it was being sold to Glencore. A separate Viterra terminal known as the "C" House was sold to Richardson at the same time. With that sale, Richardson's storage capacity in Thunder Bay increased from 208,000 metric tons to an impressive 435,000 metric tons—the port's largest grain storage capacity.

Part of the reason for Richardson's expansion in Thunder Bay—a reason that makes Gerry very happy—was a recent change in the way Canadian wheat and barley are marketed. The Canadian Wheat Board (the "CWB") was established by an act of the Canadian parliament in 1935. That act provided that all of the wheat and barley produced in the provinces of Manitoba, Saskatchewan, and Alberta, plus the Peace River District of British Columbia, had to be marketed through the CWB. Since these areas produced most of the wheat and barley grown in Canada, the CWB was, for many farmers, the only game in town. It was the only legal buyer of wheat and barley. Many farmers liked the sense that there would always be a buyer for the wheat and barley they grew. It made for a predictable, regulated structure they could count on. It also provided market power to the CWB, who could act as a single, large seller able to command a high price for the grain it was selling.

Over time, some farmers found the system too constricting. Many turned to other crops that farmers were free to sell as they thought best. But the final difficulty for the CWB was that its structure was anathema to the economic ideas of the Conservative government that came into power as the federal government of Canada in 2006. The Conservatives sympathized with the private part of the grain handling industry that found it frustrating to do business within a system that limited their economic freedom of action. Richardson is very much in that part of the industry.

The CWB didn't own any grain handling facilities. It didn't own railroads, or elevators, or shipping lines. To move the grain it purchased, it contracted with others. Its choice of companies to deal with, however, was not made on strictly economic grounds. Those choices often involved political decisions. Above all, the CWB had to operate with what it thought of as a system of "fairness" to all of the players involved.

This system is now changing. The CWB's monopoly officially ended on August 1, 2012. There is still support for the CWB and, even after August 2012, it continues to operate. (About 10 percent of the grain now flowing through Thunder Bay elevators is what is called "board grain"—grain sold through the CWB.) Supporters include many farmers who see it as protection against big agribusiness and large rail and shipping companies who might be able to manipulate transactions with individual farmers to the farmer's disadvantage. At least for a few years, those who want to use the CWB marketing system, can. The federal government committed itself to supporting the CWB for five years. After that, it is on its own, and whether it finds a way to continue or sells its marketing force to a private company is yet to be determined.

For Gerry Heinrichs, the CWB doesn't have much to offer a buyer. It has no tangible assets. All it has, in his opinion, is people who know how to fill out order forms. Now it is "balls out, go to the wall," and Gerry thinks that, in this free-market environment, good times for Richardson have arrived and the CWB will be a thing of the past.

The new driver behind the wheel is not the farmer, or government regulators, or, for that matter, grain handling companies. As Gerry says, "It's about what the customer wants." If Canadian farmers are growing the kind of grain that customers want, there will be more demand and, consequently, more producers. Even the thinking behind the Canadian Grain Act that promotes Canadian grain by insisting on what the act defines as "quality" grain doesn't necessarily make sense to him.

The Canadian Grain Act requires that wheat, when shipped, has to be "clean." That means shipped Canadian wheat can contain no more than 1 percent "foreign material," or "f.m." in elevator talk. But a customer may not care and may not want to pay the extra cost of cleaning to ensure a low f.m. Wheat shipped from the United States and other exporting nations can have a higher f.m. if that is what the buyer and seller agree, and the United States sells a lot more wheat than Canada despite the lack of this legislated "quality" feature. In short, Gerry thinks that the controls that were exercised by the CWB and through the Canadian Grain Act may better be left for producers, shippers, and customers to work out on their own.

Gerry Heinrichs also thinks that more market freedom will help ensure the future of grain elevator operations in Thunder Bay. The market for Canadian grain has shifted. Countries on the Pacific Rim are now buying more Canadian grain than European countries are buying. Pacific Rim countries have become more prosperous and, therefore, their demand for grain has increased. European Union countries are producing more grain, and crop yields in Russia and Ukraine have increased. These increases mean that there is less need to import grain from Canada and, consequently, less grain flows east through Thunder Bay.

Some specific demands, however, are steady. "Salties," ships that can sail from Thunder Bay through the St. Lawrence Seaway and across the ocean, load durum wheat in Thunder Bay for delivery in Italy where it is the crucial ingredient in pasta production. At the same time, consumers in Canada, the United States, and Europe are becoming more particular about diet and want specific kinds of grain. These grains may be organic or have other quality specifications. They are referred to as "identity-preserved grains" and they are becoming a bigger part of the grain market. Getting them to market requires particular attention. The farmer who has agreed to provide some identity-preserved grain has to ensure that it will be segregated from other grains as it moves from farm to buyer. The western Canadian elevators in Vancouver and Prince Rupert, British Columbia, are too busy to bother about the kind of handling this grain requires. But Thunder Bay has the capacity and expertise to do this job. Identity-preserved grains are likely to become a big part of the elevator business there. Gerry is "very optimistic" that Thunder Bay elevator operations will continue to do well and that the level of business they are now doing will be sustained. As for Gerry, it looks like he will be a part of that Thunder Bay grain business, at least until he "grows up" and joins his brother-in-law on the farm.

5

⚬⚬⚬

How They Work

The Richardson elevator offices may be in the same building that holds the grain, but managing an elevator and working in one are two different things. After our interview, Gerry walked me over to Ryan Fay's office. Ryan's office is in the working part of the elevators and has a bank of computers against the wall. Ryan is the elevator's operations supervisor. He is a young man who has worked at the Richardson elevator for four years. Gerry "volunteered" him to give me a tour of the elevator.

Before we left Gerry's office, Gerry had been worried whether I was dressed for an elevator tour. He thought my coat was too nice and too dark to be worn in a dusty elevator and he wondered about my shoes. I assured him that my shoes were sturdy—"sensible," as he jokingly called them. I left my coat in the office, risking the cold. Elevators aren't heated or air-conditioned. They are cold in the winter and get a little hotter in the summer. They are dusty and noisy all the time.

I had been fitted out with a hard hat and a brightly colored vest. If the weather had been better and the railroad had managed to deliver grain cars, we would have started outside at the "car shed." The name is a holdover from the days when grain arrived in boxcars. When boxcars carried grain, the grain emptied through a door in the side of the boxcar. The wooden planks that enclosed the grain behind the sliding doors of the boxcars had to be broken through before the grain ran out. Then, since there was grain left in the ends of the boxcar, "shovelers" had to get inside the boxcar and use mechanical paddles to push out the remaining grain. This was hard, dirty work and it took time. The paddles pushed the grain out of the boxcar doors, but you had to be quick in order to avoid getting pushed along with the grain or, worse yet, getting your leg tangled in the rope attached to the paddles. The paddles worked automatically and kept pulling until they got to the door.

That's all changed now. Grain arrives in Thunder Bay in waterproof, steel hopper cars with hatches in the bottom of the hopper for easy unloading. A worker runs an electrically powered rig along the track beside the hopper. Sitting inside, he uses controls to insert a device that looks like a large version of a square-head screwdriver into the hopper door mechanism and turns it to open the hatch. The same thing could be done by hand, but that's not how it is done at the Richardson elevator.

The way grain arrives at the elevator is not the only thing that has changed since the first part of the Richardson elevator was built in 1918. The elevator itself has grown. Other sections were added in 1922, 1930, and 1970. It is now an efficient, modern elevator and the way it works is typical of all but one of the Thunder Bay elevators. Still, some of the recent changes don't fit perfectly with the older parts. That misfit is obvious right from the start. Hopper cars carry more grain than boxcars—more than half again as much—but the "receiving garner" that takes the grain that pours from the hopper car was built for boxcars. Even after expansion to the limits allowed by the dimensions of the original building, the garner can't handle a full hopper load all at once. One hatch door is left closed until the conveyer belt below the garner has removed enough of the load to allow the last hatch to be opened and poured in.

Even before any hatch is opened, a more significant change in grain handling appears. When the hopper car is first pushed over the receiving garner, its brake is set and the track on which it sits lifts up. The whole hopper is being weighed. It will be weighed before and after unloading. Even though the weight and grade of the grain in the hopper has been recorded at the prairie elevator where it was loaded, those things are doubled checked in Thunder Bay. Now, although there are still a few "producer" cars that are loaded by farmers on railway spur lines they have purchased, none of those cars arrive at Richardson's Thunder Bay terminal. All of the grain is Richardson's grain—bought and paid for when it was received from the farm.

Weighing also used to be different. As each car was unloaded, the grain it contained was sent separately up an interior "leg" that lifted that carload of grain up into the elevator's workhouse. There, it was first collected in another garner. From that garner, it was released into a scale. The weight of the grain in that carload was recorded and credited to the farmer who grew it. The grain was then released and distributed to its storage place in the elevator.

A lot happens to the grain after it is unloaded and begins its travels into the elevator. Shortly after the grain heads out of the receiving garner by conveyor, a neat machine called a Woodside sampling device dips into the grain and picks up quarter-cup sized samples of grain and sends them off for testing. The grain on the conveyor then travels under large electromagnets that pick up any metal that might be in it. Nails are common and, occasionally, the odd hammer or other tool gets lifted out of the grain by the magnets. The grain from the Woodside sampler is first tested to determine its protein content and its moisture level. Then it goes through a "kicker" machine that measures the percentage of foreign material in the grain and, after that, the tester measures the percentage of kernels that are broken and whether any other type of grain is mixed in. Finally, someone takes a closer look to see if the grain has been damaged by frost or otherwise and whether or not it is discolored or carrying mold or fungus. On the basis of these tests, the grain is given a grade. Number 1 is the best and number 5 the worst. Most commercial sales deal in grain that is graded number 1 or number 2. After that, the grain is unlikely to be used for bread or other human food. Number 5 durum wheat, for example, would only be used for animal feed.

Every load of every type of grain is given a grade. The Richardson elevator handles wheat (both red and durum), barley, oats, flax, canola seed, lentils, soybeans, and peas, as well as an occasional load of canary seed. Each kind needs to be identified and given an initial grade in the hope that by handling it the right way, its grade, and therefore its value, can be increased. If you can move grain up one grade from what it was when first received from the farm by cleaning, drying, and sorting it, its value when delivered by the elevator to a customer will be greater than what the elevator company paid for it on receipt.

The Richardson terminal elevator in Thunder Bay supplies wheat to Warburtons bakery in Britain. Warburtons is an exacting customer. It requires grain that has a specified protein content and moisture level. Warburtons even insists that the grain it receives come from certain growing locations. In addition to the initial sorting and grading of grain arriving at the elevator, therefore, Ryan Fay and his crew have to know the source of the grain in order to create the exact mix of wheat that Warburtons or other customers require. Warburtons may need number 1 red, southern, Spring wheat while a pasta maker in Italy may need number 1 amber durum, northern winter wheat. Customer requirements make initial sorting, grading, and identification of the grain essential.

Since it takes time to complete the testing of the grain in each hopper car, that grain goes first from the receiving garner to a holding bin. Once its type, grade, and characteristics are determined, it can be taken into the elevator proper and distributed. To do that, it is again carried by conveyer to internal legs that lift the grain high up in the elevator to garners in the workhouse above the distribution floor. Spouts leading down from those garners can be moved around in a circle by a motorized device on the bottom of each spout. The spouts can reach a number of circular lids in the floor that can be opened under the spout to carry the grain to treatment or storage. Each has a code marked on it to show where a worker will be sending the grain. It might be sent to be cleaned, that is, to remove foreign material, or sent to dryers to remove moisture. If none of those processes are needed, the grain will be sent directly down to the bin floor for storage.

The bin floor is one floor below the distribution floor. On the bin floor, the grain will be carried to a bin that has been identified as holding that particular type and grade of grain. Any grain that has gone through the cleaners or dryers will also end up on the bin floor to be sent to its appointed storage bin. Usually, the stored grain will be held in its bin until the time comes to ship it. Back downstairs, on the computers in the control room, the grain's destination is recorded and, just to make it easier to keep track, someone also goes to the chalkboard that covers one of the office walls and marks down the kind of grain being held in each bin. A pattern of circles on the wall chart shows all of the bins in the elevator and, if there is any grain in the bin, the variety and grade is chalked in on the chart circle by circle. You can see from the chart that there are bins between the bins. Four large circular bins will necessarily create a space between them where they meet. This space is also used for grain storage, so that no space is wasted.

Ryan and I had taken the elevator up to the distribution floor. The elevator that carried us was a people-carrying elevator of the standard industrial sort—big, with a heavy wire cage behind a door that divided horizontally when it opened. Ryan lifted the iron bar hinged across the middle and pulled up on the bar to let us in. Impressive as that was, I felt disappointed. I had been hoping for a man lift. Years before, I had ridden one up through the floors of the Manitoba Pool 1 elevator in Thunder Bay. You stepped onto a moving platform about eighteen inches wide and hung on. There was no enclosing cage. You simply moved up through the floors by virtue of the belt attached to the platform you stood on. The lift operated continuously, traveling round and round through holes cut in each floor. When you got to where you wanted to go, you stepped off. When I asked Ryan whether this kind of lift had been used in the Richardson elevator, he pointed to an off-colored patch of concrete to the left of the elevator as we got off. It covered the place where the hole for the man lift once had been. This was yet another change to the way grain elevators worked. It likely wouldn't have been noticed by anyone other than by someone like me who was looking for a man lift and hoping for another ride.

The distribution floor wasn't really the "top" floor. Higher up in the workhouse were floors holding garners and scales and the machinery that made the elevator work. We had decided that we could skip those floors and the noise and danger that those machines represented. Few workers other than the mechanics who had to maintain the machines ever ventured up there.

The unvisited machines on the upper floors of the workhouse worked steadily. We could hear them powering all of the lifts, legs, and conveyors operating in the elevator. Even on a day when the elevator was operating at a low level, we still had to raise our voices to hear one another. Part of that noise came from grain running through the spouts on the distribution floor and from the conveyor belts on the bin floor below, but the workhouse machines produced a constant rumbling undertone.

The machines in the workhouse, along with the gears and belts they drive, need space. The need for that space means that the work-house extends as much as eighty feet above the top of the bins. From the outside, the workhouse looks like a distinct part of the elevator building. As I mentioned earlier when describing the appearance of a modern elevator, the workhouse is the rectangular part that sticks up above everything else. Unlike the smooth, uninterrupted walls of the bins, the workhouse contains windows that mark each floor. It may be at the end of the elevator or in the middle. There is even an elevator in Buffalo that has two workhouses, one at each end. But no matter where it is placed, at least one has to be there, since it is indispensable to making a modern elevator work.

After our visit to the distribution floor, we walked down stairs to the bin floor and stepped into a long, open gallery-like space lined with windows along the gallery walls. Light filtered through the windows and played over the dust in the air. The whole length of the floor showed row after row of square metal hatch covers stretching in straight lines to the blank, unwindowed end wall—a wall that seemed very far away. Conveyor belts ran the length of the floor toward the distant wall. One of the belts was carrying grain. About halfway down the floor, the conveyor belt bumped up over a trip machine that deflected the grain off the belt into a bin.

As we walked toward the machine, we spotted an elevator worker beside the bin receiving the grain. I was amazed by what I saw. He was flinging one arm up into the air, bringing it down and flinging it up again. Ryan had to explain. The elevator worker was not mad with dust inhalation; he was using a long-practiced method of measurement. To determine the height of grain in the bin being filled, he had thrown a heavy plastic weight down through the open hatch. That weight was attached to a long length of rope. When it landed on the top of the growing pile of grain in the bin, the worker began pulling the rope up in long sweeping strokes. At the end of each stroke, his bottom hand pinched against the rope, his top hand came down to the bottom hand and his arm swept up again. Each pull was counted in order to measure the remaining space in the bin.

This was not a new method of measurement, but nothing had been found to replace it. It was the same method used on sailing ships and the same method seen by Mark Twain on a Mississippi steamboat. A sailor would stand at the bow of a ship and throw a weighed line with regularly spaced knots ahead into the water. The water's depth was measured by the number of knots stretching down into the water as the line became vertical. The method gave Samuel L. Clemens his pen name of "Mark Twain." Before the Civil War, Clemens worked as a steamboat pilot on the Mississippi. Navigation of the shoals and sandbars of the Mississippi required posting someone at the bow end of the steamboat to throw a line to measure the depth of the water so that the pilot could avoid running aground. The depth was measured in "marks" and their number had to be called out to the pilot as the steamboat made its way along the river. A depth of two marks would be mark "twain" and Clemens, as a pilot, frequently heard the crewman responsible for checking the water's depth call out, "by the mark twain," the name that Clemens eventually adopted as a writer.

Modern devices have replaced this method of measuring water depth on ships, but none has been found to do the job in grain elevators. Efforts have been made to use more up-to-date methods in the elevator, but the weight-and-pull method has lasted. Other methods just don't work. If, for example, you try to beam a laser into a bin to determine the distance to the accumulating grain, you cannot get an accurate measure. The dust kicked up from the grain pouring into the bin gets so thick that the beam loses its way. It deflects and bounces around hopelessly and never heads straight back to the instrument taking the reading. The old way is the only way to know when the bin is filling and when the flow of grain has to be stopped before grain runs out the open hatch and spills across the floor. Ryan said that everyone who starts to work on the bin floor usually creates one spill. After that, he learns to measure more frequently. If a worker reports a floor covered with spilt grain, he is told where he can find a shovel, broom, and wheelbarrow to clean it up.

Ryan bent over the bin filling with grain to take a closer look. Kernels poured quickly off the trip machine and Ryan grabbed a handful. It was red wheat and many of the kernels were cracked or broken. He admitted that this was less than top quality wheat, probably destined for a customer in North Africa and for uses that didn't demand the highest grade of grain. This bin was close to the conveyor but I wondered how grain from one of the conveyor belts could get to the bins far from the belt and close to the outer walls. Ryan said that spouts that attached to the trip machine could reach all the way from the belt and could be moved easily on retractable wheels to the hatches of those faraway bins.

We were heading back toward the passenger elevator. Other machines were visible on the bin floor as we approached the elevator. These machines received grain from the distribution floor for cleaning and drying. Cleaners work one of two ways. A cleaning machine either sifts the grain through screens or spins it in drums. Both kinds do the same job. The cleaners remove dirt, stones, sticks, straw, stray seeds, husks, and other foreign material from the grain. The dryers work by passing the grain through hot air that removes extra moisture. Ryan noted that these machines are now used less and less in the Thunder Bay elevators. Most of the grain coming into the Thunder Bay elevators had already been cleaned and dried on the Prairies. Only about 10 percent of what the Richardson elevator receives needs to be cleaned. Even less needs to be dried. Almost none, in fact. It's better for the grain if it's dry when it leaves the Prairie elevators. The steel hopper cars that carry the grain to Thunder Bay are watertight so they keep out moisture on the way to Thunder Bay. There are still dryers in the Thunder Bay elevators and sometime canola seed—a notoriously moist and sticky grain—has to be dried, but it is not usually the case. The dirt, sticks, and stones from the cleaners get thrown away. The other refuse—essentially, plant material—is kept. This cleaning residue is called "screenings" and goes to the elevator's pellet mill to be processed into animal feed.

In an elevator, everything starts at the bottom and moves up. Joseph Dart understood that. His mechanized buckets "elevated" grain out of lake boats. Once it was elevated, the grain could be moved by gravity. Dart knew that if he could find a way to get the grain high enough, gravity would carry it down to the canal boats below. In a modern elevator such as the Richardson elevator, the same basic principle holds. The added element is the conveyor belts that move the grain horizontally through the elevator on belts powered by electricity. The movement of grain either begins in the basement or requires that the grain return there in order to move elsewhere. The grain coming in from the hopper cars moves up to the garners above the distribution floor on lift legs that are essentially the same as the ones Dart invented. If grain has to move from one bin to another, it has to run out the bottom of the bin and repeat its trip along a basement conveyor and up another lift leg. But Ryan admitted that he didn't like moving grain from one bin to another. Doing that is unusual and provides too many chances for trouble.

Ryan and everyone working in the elevator are aiming for one thing—to get the grain through the elevator and onto a ship. Grain stored in the bins is released at the bottom and carried along on as many as four different conveyors to the elevator's four shipping legs. It then travels up the shipping legs and pours down into the four loading spouts on the outside of the elevator that are positioned in the holds of a ship docked in the elevator slip. Ideally, each belt and each of the shipping legs carries an equal amount of grain. When they do, the grain trimmers supervising the loading have an easier time ensuring that the load is distributed evenly and the ship's "trim" is properly maintained.

Since the Richardson elevator has only four fixed loading spouts, they may not reach all of the holds in the ship. In that case, the ship has to move back and forth under the spouts. The boats currently operating on the Great Lakes can carry up to 25,000 metric tons of grain. Ocean ships or "salties" might be able to carry more, but they have to be careful. Traveling the St. Lawrence Seaway, all ships have to pass through the St. Mary's River going in or out of the Sault Saint Marie locks. The shipping channel in the St. Mary's River is cut through rock that, at one point, has a maximum depth of 26½ feet. If a ship's load is too heavy and the ship's draft is too deep, the ship will flounder in that rock cut.

There was more of the Richardson elevator to see in my tour, including the completely separate annex built in 1970. The annex connects to the main elevator building by a bridging passageway that stretches from the bin floor. A conveyor runs into the annex, so the annex doesn't need a separate workhouse. Therefore, no workhouse rises above the annex and it simply has a long, flat, concrete roof over the conveyor belt. As we headed toward the bridge to the annex, a worker arrived with the news that the high wind I had driven through on my way to the elevator was blowing more than snow. Pieces of the asphalt and shingle that covered the concrete roof of the annex were being lifted off and blown about into the parking lot and into the slip alongside the elevator. This news ended the tour. Ryan had his hands full with the roof problem and I was left to get back to Gerry's office for my coat.

The return trip to the parking lot was worse than the trip to the elevator. I again had to work my way down the loading dock in order to get to the van I was driving. I was feeling a bit rattled by the wind and the pieces of roof that were flying through the air and I took a moment to check whether I had everything before starting the van. As I did, I noticed it was strangely cold and breezy. I looked over my shoulder and saw that a large piece of roofing material had hit and smashed the back window of the van. It was a direct hit. Nothing but the window was damaged. I decided that the damage was my lookout and began to drive away. I got about a quarter of a mile from the elevator to a point where the road turned right and crossed the railroad tracks. There was an open field on the right and the snow had drifted across the field and piled deeply across the road and tracks. I looked for the place where the drift was shallowest and gave it try. About halfway through, the van stuck in the drift. It didn't seem like a good idea to get in any deeper and to be out in the storm on my own, so I slowly backed out and returned to the elevator.

By this time, there was a general alert in the elevator. I managed once more to cross the end of the parking lot and got to the loading dock where I was happy to be beckoned into a door that had been opened into the elevator basement. The worker who called to me was amazed that I was walking around without a hard hat while pieces of the annex roof were flying through the air. I followed him through the basement and up the stairs to Gerry Heinrichs's office. Gerry didn't seem that concerned about either the wind or my van's rear window, but agreed to my request that I be led down the road and through the snowdrifts. My worker friend offered to lead the way in his pickup truck and Gerry gave his blessing. On the way to the parking lot, I again avoided the loading dock by taking the basement route and I hoped for the best as I made my way from the basement door to the van. I arrived at the van without being hit by a piece of flying roof and waited for my trailblazing guide. His Dodge Ram truck had no trouble with the drifts and I followed in his tracks through to the main road. Thunder Bay is a beautiful place on a warm day when the sun is shining on Lake Superior and a gentle breeze is blowing, but if you come in April, be prepared for winter.

6

✥

Grain Dust Stories

I remember my father coming home from work in the elevator. When he walked through the door, I could smell the sweet smell of grain dust on his clothes. Dust is grain's constant companion. Even shiny flaxseeds that look so clean and bright kick up dust as they move. For most elevator workers, grain dust becomes an unnoticed part of the elevator's atmosphere. It gets under overalls easily and onto regular work clothes. It piles up on beams and window ledges. It hangs in the air.

Grain elevator workers wear masks only for the dirtiest jobs and even then, when my father was working, the masks were just layers of cotton held against the nose and mouth by a flexible metal frame secured around the head with an elastic cord. The usual attitude is a casual disregard of the dust. Elevators workers think it enough to wash it down with a couple of beers at the end of a shift. That formula doesn't work for everyone. Some workers are more sensitive to dust than others. While itchy red patches around the neck and at the elbows and knees are common, for a few, dust causes serious trouble. I was one of those. I only lasted two weeks at the Searle elevator before the dust itch got so bad I had to quit.

Dust isn't just annoying; it can be deadly. From 1988 to 1997, inclusive, there were 129 reported explosions in flourmills and elevators around the world. If grain dust in high enough concentrations is confined in a space where there is a source of ignition, it will explode. There are YouTube videos demonstrating dust explosions. Even an explosion fueled by only one teaspoon of flour is impressive.

But those demonstrations are nothing when compared to a full-scale flourmill or elevator disaster. When the Washburn "A" Mill in Minneapolis, Minnesota, exploded in 1878, eighteen workers were killed and two nearby buildings were damaged. The Washburn is only one in a long line. Elevators and flourmills had blown up for many years before 1878. The first record of such an event was in 1785. An Italian flourmill exploded that year. There have been many dust explosions since then and they continue to this day.

Air, fuel (i.e., dust), containment and an ignition source are all that is needed for grain dust to explode. Herb Daniher, a former elevator worker and now a staff representative for the United Steelworkers, told me a story from his days working in a Thunder Bay elevator. He was working in the elevator office. Unlike other parts of the elevator, the office had a heater and a window air conditioner—not for the comfort of those who worked in the office, but to keep the office temperature comfortable for the computers. Often neither was used. The office was not as dusty as other parts of the elevator, but dust still collected there, particularly on and inside the switch for the heater. The heater had not been used for quite a while, but one cold, rainy day someone decided to flick the switch for some heat. He got more than he expected. An electrical arc within the switch supplied a spark. When the spark hit the dust in the switch, the dust ignited. That started a chain reaction. The switch blew off the wall and the airborne dust in the room joined in the explosion. Just another day at the office!

No place in the elevator is more sheltered from grain dust than the elevator offices. If enough dust can collect there, the explosive potential of the rest of the elevator is many times greater. Of the elements needed for an explosion, only two can be controlled: the amount of dust and the existence of an ignition source. Most modern elevators have dust extractor systems that attempt to remove enough grain dust from the air inside the elevator so that dust can't build up to dangerous levels. There are also many work and safety rules that try to eliminate sparks and flames. Despite these efforts, however, elevators still blow up. On October 29, 2011, the Bartlett Grain Company in Atchison, Kansas, exploded. Six people were killed.

On August 8, 1945, the front page of the Fort William *Daily Times Journal* carried side-by-side pictures of two explosions. One was a picture of the atomic bomb blast at Hiroshima on August 6. The other was a picture of the twisted metal of a workhouse addition under construction at the Saskatchewan Pool 5 elevator in the Current River area of Port Arthur. The explosion that caused this damage had happened the day before. Strangely, wartime needs had caused both events. The scale was vastly different, of course, but arguments from necessity figured in both. Dropping the atomic bomb was argued as the only way to end to war with Japan. Saving steel for wartime use was agreed to be the only way to carry on the Canadian war effort. Because steel was scarce during the war years, Pool 5 was unable to have dust removal equipment manufactured and installed. That wartime sacrifice produced conditions that led to the Pool 5 explosion.

The lack of adequate dust removal equipment might not have been the sole reason for the explosion. There was a lake boat docked by the elevator taking on a load of refuse screenings. At the time, the Canadian government had banned the use of screenings for domestic use, so they were stored until there was enough to justify a shipment to the United States. Screenings are the residue from the cleaning machines and they tend to be particularly dusty. Since the screenings had to be moved from a bin that opened in the elevator basement and since they then had to travel by conveyor belt to a shipping leg, they had plenty of chances to kick up clouds of dust on the way. That dust cloud would have been particularly dense in the basement. According to the official investigation of the accident, an exposed light bulb in the basement was the source of ignition. The secondary explosion traveled up through the elevator, blowing out walls, doors, and windows and smashing the scaffolding that had held the men working on the addition.

Once the scaffolding was blown away, the dead and injured workmen on or near it were isolated 125 feet above the ground and thirty feet from the nearest building. Firemen and rescue workers hurried to the elevator site. Private Bruce Cudmore of the Veterans Guard of Canada, together with other recently discharged navy men, rigged a rope and bosun's chair across the gap and managed to bring the injured to safety and to recover the dead. In all, twenty-two people died as the result of the explosion and more than thirty-five were injured. The elevator was rebuilt the next year. Rubble from the explosion was used to fortify the slip wall that ran between Pool 5 and the Richardson elevator next door. The rebuilt elevator was rechristened Saskatchewan Pool 4B, and thus officially paired with Saskatchewan Pool 4A which sat beside it. Seven years later, Pool 4A took its turn to blow.

Bob Speak was seventeen and working on a construction site in Thunder Bay in 1951. The job paid a dollar an hour, but it was hard work pushing 150-pound buckets filled with concrete around the work site. When he heard that the Saskatchewan Pool elevators were hiring, he got himself to the hiring office at 9 a.m. on August 24, 1951. He knew the elevator job paid one cent an hour less than his construction job, but it did not involve pushing heavy buckets of concrete. The fellow doing the hiring felt his muscles and asked him his age. He said, "Seventeen." "Oh," the elevator man said, "You've got to be eighteen to work in the elevator." A few seconds passed and the man asked again, "How old did you say you were?" Bob gave the right answer this time. He was told to report to Pool 4A in the Current River section of Port Arthur that same day at noon.

Bob had been working at Pool 4A for a little over a year. It was noon on December 11, 1952, and half of the workers were out of the elevator on their lunch break. Bob, unfortunately, was not among them. Shortly after noon, when the elevator blew up, the force of the explosion threw Bob across the floor and into the wall. His clothes were set on fire and the hair was burned off his face, but he was alive. His first thought was to get out a door and jump into Lake Superior but the blast had jammed the doors closed. His second thought was to run out the end of the building. When he began running, he was joined by a fellow worker named Steve. As the two of them ran away from the building, it began to rain bricks. One of the bricks hit Steve in the back of the head and he went down with other bricks piling on top of him. There was no helping Steve; he was dead. Bob kept running down an embankment and over some boards that had been torn out of a boxcar door. The grain between the boards acted like ball bearings and the top board flew out from under his feet. Down he went, catching his mitt on a nail sticking out of one the boards and wrenching his arm so badly it was broken. He got up, holding his arm, and kept running. He reached a shed where he got help putting out the smoldering fire on his clothes. From there, he was sent with other injured workers to the Port Arthur General Hospital.

At the hospital, a whole floor was devoted to those injured in the explosion. Bob considers himself lucky to have been treated by Dr. Baker, a former army doctor, who bandaged his burned face and hands and ordered a nurse to soak his bandages with saltwater every hour. The result was that, when the bandages were finally removed, his skin looked like new. That saltwater treatment was unknown before World War II. British military doctors had noticed that the burns of pilots whose planes had crashed into the sea healed better than others. They concluded that the exposure to saltwater had helped heal the burns and adopted the treatment used by Dr. Baker.

Many others who were burned in the elevator explosion had their burns treated with ointment. That didn't work so well. In fact, those burned workers looked so ghastly that all of the mirrors were removed from the hospital floor on which the injured workers were treated. The doctors had decided that the effect of their burns was so bad that they would not be able to bear the sight of themselves.

Oddly, Bob regretted losing only one thing. He was wearing his hockey jersey to work the day of the explosion. It was burned by the blast and it had to be cut off him to treat his wounds. Between those two things, it was destroyed. He regretted the loss of that jersey for a long time. Others might have sought another line of work after they had been through an elevator explosion. Bob didn't. He worked in the Thunder Bay Saskatchewan Pool elevators until he retired.

Bob was retired when he recorded his account of working in the Saskatchewan Pool elevators. I wanted to talk to somebody about what it is like working in an elevator today, so I met with Cody Hubert. Cody is twenty-six, and he has been working in the Mission Terminal elevator for four years. The Mission Terminal elevator is located near the mouth of the Kam River in the part of Thunder Bay that used to be Fort William. It sits, in fact, beside the former Grand Trunk Pacific Elevator and it was once the Searle Elevator— the one I had worked in. He is a big guy with a beard and looks like he would have no trouble doing a full day's work. At the elevator, he works outside most of the time driving the switch engine that moves hopper cars in and out of the car shed and maintaining that engine. Since hopper cars have replaced boxcars, there is no need to have workers shovel the grain from the corners of the car any more as they did when Bob Speak worked at Pool 4A. After the grain from the hopper cars gets into the elevator, it moves around much as it has for decades. But there is one big difference between the picture that Bob Speak paints of life in the Thunder Bay elevators and Cody's experience. Cody has far fewer fellow workers.

When Bob started working for Saskatchewan Pool, there were more than two thousand people on the work list for the Thunder Bay elevators. There are probably closer to 250 workers now. Part of that reduction is easily explained; Thunder Bay has fewer elevators to work in. But other reasons for the reduction are not so easy to pinpoint. Some jobs have been eliminated. There is no more need for shovelers to get grain out of the corners of the boxcars and, since there is less grain that needs to be cleaned or dried, fewer workers are needed to run those machines.

The elevators now operate more efficiently and more machines can be run from a computer. The grain also moves faster. The conveyor belts used now are wider, move more quickly and are more pitched. The pitch may be the most important change. Belts used to be almost flat. That meant that it was more likely that grain would move toward the edge of the moving belts and spill out of the shallow trough. Now the rollers are angled higher along the sides of the belt to create a deeper trough for the grain. This allows more grain to stay on the belt and the belt can move more quickly. Despite these reasons, it still seems strange to an outsider that such large structures can be run by so few workers. Although it is an extreme example, the Western 10 elevator in the Westfort area of Thunder Bay is run by five people, including the owner, Maurice Mailhot. The whole elevator has a permanent staff of four workers, one in the office and three in the elevator proper. These four people run a large elevator, and only when a boat needs to be loaded are extra temporary workers hired.

Cody acknowledges that there are differences at the Mission Terminal elevator that distinguish it in other ways. It is the only nonunion elevator in Thunder Bay, and that means those who work there have to be more flexible. The Mission Terminal elevator also handles more "board" grain for the Canadian Wheat Board than other Thunder Bay elevators. Since the CWB is handling less and less of the grain produced on the Canadian Prairies, less may be destined for the Mission Terminal. Cody estimates the Mission elevator work force to be around fifty. That is a comparatively large number for a Thunder Bay elevator. The Mission Terminal elevator runs only one shift, and even then it furloughs workers for a week at a time when grain shipments are light. Cody doesn't mind the occasional week off. He can charge that time against his vacation allowance, and there is always plenty of work to do around home.

Elevators differ, but wherever it is handled, grain acts like grain. Although Cody works outside most of the time, he knows the jobs that need to be done inside. There is one that both he and Bob Speak know to be particularly hard and dangerous. It is a job where the dust is thickest. Sometimes a bin has to be cleaned and, to do that, a worker gets lowered into the bin through a hatch at the top. He is strapped into a chair that spins and swings on the rope holding it as it travels farther and farther down into the bin. The swinging is part of the job. The chair has to swing back and forth so that the worker in it can reach the bin walls. Grain clings to bin walls and has to be knocked off to clean the bin. The worker cleaning the bin can only get to the walls if the chair is allowed to swing close to them.

It may sound like fun, but it isn't. This is one job where a dust mask is essential. The dust can get so thick it is hard to breath and impossible to see. Sometimes there is a serious problem when the grain won't flow out from the bottom of the bin. When sticky grain such as canola refuses to run out of the funnel at the bottom, the worker cleaning the bin has to get out of his chair onto the grain to poke it down with his feet. At this point, the job gets dangerous. If the grain begins to flow, as it should, onto the conveyor moving below the bin, it can suck the worker down with it. Even though he is still attached to the rope that lowered his chair, there is a lot of stretch in the rope and if he doesn't manage to get someone to close the bottom of the bin or get the conveyor stopped, he can be pulled down into the grain and drown—rope and all.

Engineers call grain a "semi liquid." Each kernel is solid, but it piles and flows like water. Being pulled down into grain is like going underwater. Such "drownings" happen more often on farms than in elevators. National Public Radio reported in March 2013 that 660 U.S. farmers and workers had suffocated in grain since 1964. Elevator workers wear safety harnesses and have other safety procedures in place when they get on a pile of grain in a bin and start doing what is called, "walking down the grain." On farms, younger farm workers think less about the dangers. In 2010 in Mt. Carroll, Illinois, three teenaged boys were trapped by the quicksand effect produced by grain running out of a bin. Two died. The youngest was fourteen.

The life-threatening task of walking down grain at the bottom of a bin, however, is not considered the worst job in the elevator. That distinction is earned by the delightfully named job of "banjoing." Most elevator bins have funnel-shaped bottoms, but some, like those that were in Thunder Bay's Pool 6, are flat. All the grain doesn't run out of a flat-bottomed bin. When all that can run out has been emptied, there is still a lot around the sides. Pulling the remaining grain to the opening in the center of the bin is banjoing. The banjo has strings, of course—heavy rope strings attached to a board made of steel. Two players are needed for this banjo and getting ready to play is the worst part. The device is lowered to the bottom of the bin. Then the two people who are to move the grain have to climb down the bin wall from the top to get to their instrument. There are iron rungs forming ladders along the bin wall from top to bottom, but not all of them are firmly in the wall. It is a fall of more than one hundred feet from the top of the bin to the bottom, and workers have been known to quit on the spot when told it was their job to climb down and start playing the banjo. At the bottom, each worker grabs a "string" and pulls. The steel board then moves the grain along the flat bin floor into the open hatch. That's hard work, but, compared to climbing down into the bin, it's gravy.

You would never know from elevator workers that work in a grain elevator is dangerous. Cody told me about a recent explosion in the Mission Terminal. It blew a hole in the roof of the housing above the bins. He said he was sorry for the injuries it caused, but he didn't seem to feel threatened. At times, that lack of concern is hard to understand. After the Saskatchewan Pool 5 explosion, investigators recommended that smoking be banned in Thunder Bay grain elevators, but the workers resisted. Ryan Fay admitted on my tour of the Richardson elevator that when they tried to ban smoking in his elevator, they found that workers would sneak off to secluded spots to smoke without taking the danger of an explosion into account. Richardson's management finally concluded that it was better to designate a safe smoking room for workers rather than try to enforce a prohibition that could lead to someone tossing a cigarette butt into a remote corner.

Dust explosions are, without doubt, the biggest danger in a grain elevator, but some other strange and unusual dangers exist. For example, the whole building may decide to move. It's not a danger often mentioned, but Ogilvie's elevator in the part of Fort William called "Westfort" slipped into the Kam River in 1906, just two years after it was built. The Ogilvie elevator bins remained largely upright and most of the grain in the bins was successfully removed, but the United Grain Growers elevator in Port Arthur wasn't so lucky. On September 24, 1959, the storage annex of the United Grain Growers elevator slid off its foundation and fell into Lake Superior. In all, a total of more than two hundred bins, large and small, containing two and a half million bushels of grain crashed into the lake. The annex's plunge produced a minor tidal wave that caused havoc in the Port Arthur harbor. Still, like Bob Speak, the United Grain Growers elevator and its workers carried on. Working in an elevator may be dangerous, but those who work there still think it's a good job.

7

❧

Union Battles

Late in his life Woody Guthrie lived on Mermaid Avenue in Brooklyn. He wasn't performing any more, but he still wrote songs. One of them was a union song that his daughter, Nora Guthrie, arranged to have recorded after his death. It was called "I Guess I Planted" and the chorus paid tribute to early union organizers and recognized the benefits that unions had won for workers:

> Union song, union battled
> All added up, won us all what we got now

That wasn't a song that workers could sing when lake boats first arrived at Dart's elevator in Buffalo. Dart's elevator might have been inspired by Oliver Evans's automated flourmill but, unlike Evans's mill, Dart's elevator couldn't run without workers. Workers were needed the most at the very first step in the process. When a lake boat loaded with grain docked beside Dart's elevator, a mechanical "marine leg" extended out of the elevator and was lowered into the boat's hold. The way a marine leg operates was described earlier, but it bears repeating. Buckets attached to a mechanically driven belt moved around rollers at the bottom and top of the belt. As the belt moved, the buckets scooped up grain from the hold and "elevated" it into the elevator building. There wasn't much for anyone to do when the marine leg first began scooping up grain. The grain in the hold would run unassisted toward the leg and be carried up, a bucket at a time. This would continue until the marine leg got to the bottom of the hold. At that point, there would still be plenty of grain lying piled up in the corners. The marine leg had limited movement. To remove the remaining grain, someone had to get into the hold and push it toward the marine leg so that it could be lifted out.

Scooper Tales

The Buffalo workers who pushed, shoveled, and swept grain from the corners of a ship's hold into the buckets on the marine leg were known as "scoopers." They were the precursors of the Thunder Bay shovelers who moved grain out of the corners of boxcars in the car sheds of the Thunder Bay elevators. Both performed a similar task and both jobs were dirty, dusty, and difficult. But the jobs were also essential. Neither boat nor boxcar could be unloaded without them. The men who captained the lake boats carrying grain to Buffalo knew that they couldn't get their boat unloaded and on its way again unless a gang of scoopers could be found to get all the grain out of the boat when it docked at a Buffalo elevator.

Initially, it was the captain's job to find those scoopers, but that wasn't an easy thing to do from the water. The captains who found themselves with this problem solved it by finding intermediaries in Buffalo who could round up the needed scoopers and send them to the elevator ready to go to work when the ship arrived. The intermediaries who always had men on hand were Buffalo saloonkeepers.

The Buffalo elevators were built on the Buffalo waterfront and along the Buffalo River. The First Ward bordered that area. Its residents were largely immigrant Irish who needed work. Those Irish immigrants who came to Buffalo before the middle of the nineteenth century found it hard. Wages were so low that the families of working men were near starvation. In 1849, Irish laborers went on strike for a raise in wages from sixty-two and a half to seventy-five cents a day. To prevent a threat to their strike from scabs, the Irish laborers lined the towpath of the Erie Canal armed with pitchforks and kept the scabs from reaching town. This uprising became known as the "Tow-path Rebellion." It had some success, but later efforts to raise wages on the docks and railways often involved violence that alienated public sympathy, which, in turn, meant that pay and working conditions didn't improve. For the scoopers, conditions were particularly bad.

Significant troubles arose from the hiring system that had put saloonkeepers in charge of deciding who would be chosen to unload grain on the Buffalo waterfront. The saloonkeepers of the First Ward could provide needed scoopers and, as they settled into the role of labor suppliers, they became recognized as, and were called, "bosses." But these bosses remained saloonkeepers while they recruited and supplied workers and this dual role produced unhappy effects. The workers given scooper jobs were most likely to be those who spent their time and money at the bosses' bars.

Saloonkeepers often owned boardinghouses where young, unmarried Irish lads tended to live on their arrival in the United States. For a saloonkeeper who was also a boardinghouse landlord, it made good sense to ensure that these same young men got the scooper jobs, since they paid for room and board in the houses owned by the bosses and spent their time and money in the bosses' drinking establishments. Captains paid the bosses directly for the work done by the workers that the bosses supplied, so a boss could deduct rent owed and bar bills straight from a worker's wages. Little of the pay earned by the workers ended up in their hands. Even worse, married men with homes and families to support didn't get hired as frequently as younger, unmarried men because they were likely to want to collect their pay and use it for family needs rather than having it taken to discharge debts owed the boss.

This underlying hiring system seemed bound to be challenged and, in the process, it pitted two antagonists against one another who were straight out of central casting. In the black corner, wearing white trunks was William "Fingy" Conners, a tough kid from Louisiana Street with a taste for making money any way he could. In the white corner, wearing clerical black trunks was Father James E. "Jimmy" Quigley, a handsome priest with a love for the Catholic,

Irish families of Buffalo's First Ward. The fight went a number of rounds and didn't end until 1899.

These two opponents made for an interesting fight card. "Fingy" had paid a price for his nickname. When he was a young kid, he dared a playmate to cut off one of his fingers. His mate obliged, and young Conners ran home with his hand in the air shouting, "My fingy! My fingy!" Conners may have concluded that this episode gave him a lifelong privilege to hurt others. Jimmy, on the other hand, was a model boy, popular, talented, and kind—as suits a future priest.

Fingy Conners had dropped out of school at eleven and eventually went to work as a longshoreman on the Buffalo docks at seventeen. By the time he was twenty, his sister, mother, and father had died and he had inherited his father's bar and rooming house at 193 Louisiana Street, just up from the Ohio Turning Basin on the Buffalo River. Fingy quickly saw the profit potential in the scooper hiring system and set about becoming the *capo di tutti capi* of saloon bosses. By 1885, he had begun monopolizing the supply of dockworkers through an exclusive contract to supply workers to unload all of the cargo from the Union Steamboat Company ships coming into Buffalo. Soon after, he expanded this arrangement to cover the unloading of all grain shipments to Buffalo. He had won these contracts at the expense of workers. Shippers dealt with him because he kept the shippers' costs low. Fingy managed to do this by holding down the wages of workers.

At the same time that Fingy was consolidating his power and authority, another First Ward boy was rising to prominence. On February 24, 1897, Father James E. Quigley was consecrated as the third Bishop of Buffalo at the young age of forty-one. He had been born in Canada to Irish immigrant parents who moved to Rochester, New York, a few years after he was born. When Jimmy was ten, his parents sent him to live with his uncle in Buffalo, a priest who was the pastor of Immaculate Conception Church. Jimmy was a handsome young man who became a star student and athlete at St. Joseph's Collegiate. Instead of attending West Point as he originally planned, he made a sudden decision to become a Catholic priest. He studied for the priesthood in Europe and probably had the talent to succeed in the Vatican hierarchy, but he chose to return to America and soon became a rising star in the Buffalo diocese.

Before Father Quigley became a bishop, he served as the rector of St. Bridget's in the First Ward. In his short tenure there, he came to love the people of the First Ward. When he became bishop, he also became a champion of the First Ward's Irish working class.

When Conners took control of grain handling operations in Buffalo, a scooper earned an average of $4.90 a day. Once he was in charge, Fingy fixed a scooper's pay at twenty-eight cents an hour. Scoopers worked ten hour days, so this change cut their average pay in half. The scoopers had a union, but in order to prevent a union protest, Conners had inserted his handpicked cronies into the leadership of Grain Handlers Local 51 and these leaders had the union adopt the new pay scale. Most of the scoopers who were members of Local 51 rebelled and set up a rival union, Local 109, operating out of the saloon of Patrick "P. J." McMahon on Elk Street. Trouble started on April 30, 1899, when Fingy sent a gang of men to destroy McMahon's saloon. From that point on, it was union against union. The choice facing workers was to go to work at a lowered wage through Local 51 or to hold out for a better deal with Local 109.

Local 109 did not go unaided. St. Bridget's church was made available to the members of that local and the members assembled there for a meeting. Part way through the meeting, Bishop Quigley arrived to cheers from the scoopers. He made the Local 109 strikers' cause a cause for the Catholic Church and forbade all Irish Catholic grain handling workers from working for Conners. Each side had supporters. Fingy Conners could still dispense patronage to loyalists as long as he held the contract with the Lake Carriers Association that gave him control of grain unloading in Buffalo. The strikers had the backing of the Catholic Church as well as the seemingly unlikely support of Republican Congressman Rowland B. Mahany.

Mahany had grown up just outside the First Ward and his life had taken a different course from that of most First Ward residents. He had attended Hobart College and Harvard and was destined to become the first U.S. Secretary of Labor. Despite his privileges, he carried with him an affection for the working-class Irish of Buffalo.

He also had a deep dislike of Fingy Conners. When Mahany ran for Congress, his candidacy had been viciously opposed by two local newspapers, the *Courier* and the *Enquirer*. Both of those newspapers were owned by Fingy Conners, and Conners had personally called for their attacks on Mahany. Whether affection or animosity motivated Mahany's action, his support of Local 109 influenced the more established residents of Buffalo to side with the scoopers in ways that might otherwise have been unlikely.

Local 109 called a strike, and Fingy Conners had trouble rounding up strikebreakers. He tried to hire local Polish and Italian immigrants, but they sided with the strikers. He finally had to look outside Buffalo to New York City in the East and Cincinnati in the West. At first he appeared to succeed, but when the imported workers arrived in Buffalo and realized that they had been hired as strikebreakers, many defected. Striking First Ward residents then put up these workers in their own homes after they had declined to work for Conners.

Conners then turned to violence. He sent his supporters on a mission to intimidate the strikers but the strikers fought back. Shots were fired and Conners's crony William Kennedy was killed. Conners protested the strikers' violence through his newspapers, but he was losing ground and Bishop Quigley publicly urged the strikers to avoid further violence. The bishop promoted the aims of the strike through local Catholic publications, and his urging that the strikers take a nonviolent course helped prevent public opinion from turning against the strikers.

Fingy saw that he had to do something before the whole game was lost. Freight handlers in Buffalo had joined the strike and the International Seamen's Union threatened to join in as well. The president of the International Longshoremen's Association had visited Buffalo several times to speak in favor of the strikers and railway, coal, and iron industry workers had expressed their sympathy.

Even Conners's natural allies were slipping away. The Lake Carriers Association started negotiating with the strikers despite its contract with Conners because shipping had backed up across the Great Lakes. Two weeks into the strike there were 3.6 million bushels of grain waiting to be unloaded from forty-three ships sitting in Lake Erie outside Buffalo while elevators in Duluth held twenty million bushels of grain waiting to be shipped to Buffalo.

But a long strike would have been hard on the workers too, so the strikers settled for a wage of forty-nine cents an hour. In return, Conners agreed to hire only workers who were members of Local 109. He also agreed that workers would be paid where they worked and not through a saloon boss. Connor and other bosses would no longer control the money that the scoopers earned. When the strike ended, the scoopers were getting essentially the same pay they had been receiving a year before the strike began, but that wasn't so bad. It restored the cut in pay that Connors had forced on Local 51, and the pay was the best to be had on the Buffalo docks.

On my last trip to Buffalo, I looked for the Scoopers Union Hall. The address I had was 110 Louisiana Street. Louisiana Street is an easy connection from the first exit off the skyway heading south out of downtown Buffalo. I slowly counted down the house numbers as I drove down the street toward the Buffalo River until I got to 112. Next to it, where the Scoopers Hall was supposed to be, I found an empty lot. I felt sad that it was empty. I had hoped for some sort of tangible connection with the scoopers and with the Great Strike of 1899. After all, that was when the scoopers could have started to sing about the union that had "won us all what we got now." While they were singing, they would, of course, also have to tip their hats to Bishop Quigley and Congressman Mahany.

A Different Union Tale

Thunder Bay union history took a different course. The earliest Thunder Bay unions were linked directly to the railway. By 1891, four railway operating unions had been formed. These unions had even managed to achieve recognition by the railroads, despite the vigorous opposition of the Canadian Pacific Railway to any form of union organization. Others who worked for the CPR in related occupations had more difficulty. CPR freight and grain handlers formed the Fort William Labour Union in 1897. The president and vice president of this union worked as grain handlers in the CPR's Elevator B and the union secretary worked in the CPR freight yards. The organization was never recognized by the CPR and didn't last long. It backed a candidate for election to municipal office in Fort William, but that candidate lost. The union made no effort to affiliate with any larger international labor organization such as the American Federation of Labor. If it had, the link might have helped to launch the union successfully, but it simply disappeared. There are no records of its existence after 1899.

Other unionizing efforts followed and were again led by an elevator worker, although this time it was a worker involved with elevator construction rather than elevator operation. Harry A. Bryan was a radical socialist and a friend of Eugene Debs, the founder of the American Socialist Party. Bryan had moved from southern Ontario to Cleveland, Ohio, to work on Cleveland's Electric Street Railway Company. He led a strike against the company in 1899 that succeeded only in getting him blacklisted, and he had to move with his family to Dorian, near Thunder Bay, because he couldn't get work in the United States. His unionizing activity didn't stop when he moved to Thunder Bay. He organized the Barnett and Record workers who were building Elevator D into Local 53 of the International Bridge and Structural Iron Workers. He subsequently brought the workers building the CPR's steel Elevator E into the union and in 1903 he succeeded, partly through local political and public support, in winning a substantial wage increase and recognition of the union from Macdonald Engineering Company, the contractor building Elevator E.

Bryan's strike also succeeded because of the class loyalty shown by strikebreakers who were brought to Thunder Bay by the Macdonald Company. After the strikebreakers arrived by train, they realized what they were being asked to do and refused. Just as in Buffalo, the strikebreakers were then housed and fed by the Local 53 workers.

This class loyalty would often be tested in later Thunder Bay strikes and, unfortunately, it didn't always hold. One reason for this was revealed by the administrative structure that had been adopted by the short-lived Fort William Labor Union. In addition to its three elected officers, the union established an executive committee. Six of the committee members were to be of British origin and three others represented Hungarian (that is, "Slavic"), Italian, and Finnish workers, respectively. Evidently, Thunder Bay workers felt both an ethnic and class identity. This was admirable as long as the loyalties weren't at odds. There were signs from the beginning that they could easily come into conflict. The imbalance in representation on the executive committee already showed a potential division between those who considered themselves British and, therefore, proper Canadians associated with the founders of the country, and those of other nationalities who could be, and were, labeled as "foreigners."

Ethnicity played an ugly role in Thunder Bay's most dramatic workers' struggle. The CPR freightyards were located in the East End of Fort William, almost exactly on the spot where the North West Company had built its fur trading fort. The East End had been heavily settled by what the local papers called "foreign" workers. Many of those immigrants worked in the nearby CPR freight yard. Two hundred Greeks and almost an equal number of Italians plus a few Slavs and Finns did the heavy work in the freight yard. They worked eighteen hour days when there were boats to unload for seventeen and a half cents an hour. A bonus of a penny an hour was paid to workers who made themselves available for work right up to the end of the shipping season. The freightyard also employed "checkers" who kept track of the goods being moved through the freightyard and the hours worked by those who did the unloading. Almost all of the checkers were what the Fort William Union would have identified as "British."

On August 9, 1909, a committee led by Bosco Dominico, an Italian and, therefore, one of the foreign workers, called a strike. The CPR was indignant and expressed surprise that workers who were given the opportunity to work eighteen hours a day for eight months and earn a $30 bonus at the end of the shipping season would want more, or that the long hours and the daily battle for a place among those chosen to work would be a problem.

On August 12, the CPR responded with an action that insti-gated what has been called "the bloodiest labor riot ever in Canada." The CPR brought in strikebreakers and resisted negotiation with any union representative. To protect the strikebreakers, thirty heavily armed CPR police guards arrived from Winnipeg just as the strikebreakers arrived from Montreal. News of the guards' arrival brought striking workers and their families to the freightyard. The CPR police were warned by the workers not to leave their quarters, but these warnings were ignored. When the CPR police emerged, a gunfight began. No one was killed, but four CPR policemen and between twenty and thirty strikers, plus two bystanders, were wounded. The CPR police retreated before the strikers and barricaded themselves in a bunkhouse. After negotiations proved impossible, the mayor of Fort William, despite his pro-labor sympathies, read the Riot Act and called out the military. The situation was deemed so serious that additional regular troops were brought in from Winnipeg. The East End was blockaded and houses were searched for weapons.

When the French Canadian workers who were brought in by the CPR to break the strike discovered what was being asked of them, many refused to go to work and 150 of them walked off the job. The mayor of Fort William, on the promise of a fair settlement to be brokered by conciliators operating under the terms of federal labor legislation, persuaded the workers to return to work. It would be satisfying to say that this began a process that was fair, but it must not have seemed so to many freight handlers. The raise recommended by the conciliation board was small and work conditions remained unchanged. The Greek workers were singled out by the British checkers as the most dangerous among the strikers and by the CPR as the most militant. When the 1909 strike ended, the CPR resisted rehiring them. At the beginning of the 1910 shipping season, the CPR refused outright to hire any Greek workers.

The CPR also redoubled its resistance to the International Longshoremen's Association's efforts to unionize the freight handlers. Strike leaders were punished in the courts while the CPR police whose presence provoked the August 12 riot went uncharged. Public opinion had been turned against the workers by the local newspapers. The Greek workers, in particular, were stigmatized and all of the strikers were described as "violent criminals." It was not until the mid-1930s that the freight handlers in Fort William were represented by a permanent union organization. No triumphant union songs were sung in the CPR freight yards for many years.

Although the grain handlers union was not among the first of the unions organized in Thunder Bay, the grain handlers didn't need to wait as long as the freight handlers. The first recorded agreement between Thunder Bay Local 934 of the International Longshoremen's Association and elevator owners was dated June 1, 1917. I don't know of any reason for the delay in organizing.

By the time I arrived at work in the Searle Elevator, none of the ethnic divisions that had bedeviled the CPR freight handlers in Thunder Bay were evident in the elevator. There was a notion that, very early on, work in the Thunder Bay elevator was the province of Scots, but Scottish names were no more heard by me than Italian, Finnish, and Ukrainian names.

Today's Union Issues

Times have changed, and when I arrived at the Lakehead Labour Centre for my meeting with Tom Hamilton and Herb Daniher, I was introduced to a completely different set of modern labor problems. Tom is an elected officer of Lodge 650 of the Thunder Bay grain handlers' union. Lodge 650 is an affiliate of the United Steelworkers union and Herb is the representative for the Steelworkers in northwestern Ontario. Ten different industries are associated with the Steelworkers in the area that Herb covers. It puzzled me how grain handling and steel manufacturing fit together, but Herb explained that the United Steelworkers union had developed and expanded through mergers with many different union organizations and now includes workers in many fields, including communications, health care, and education. Beyond that, it made sense for a smaller local to affiliate with a large, international labor organization that can provide it with access to information and political heft in order to further local aims.

Both Tom and Herb had worked in the elevators and knew the working conditions and dangers of elevators firsthand. Tom knew what it was like to hang tethered in a chair swinging from one side of a bin to the other as you cleaned a bin through dust so thick that you could not see your hand in front of your face. He had seen workers pass out from the strange gasses that were produced in the bins being cleaned and knew of workers who had been caught and buried in grain. Both Tom and Herb knew what it was like to banjo a bin and Herb had been in the elevator office when grain dust in a light switch ignited, blowing the switch off the wall and spreading the explosion to the rest of the office.

Tom had heard a witness's story of the explosion of grain dust that had collected in the crawl space leading from the garner receiving grain from a hopper car. When the dust exploded it blasted from the crawl space like balled lightning. From these stories it is easy to understand the union's concern with safety issues, but I discovered that other issues required insight into the economic and political considerations that had altered working conditions in the Thunder Bay elevators.

During World War II, elevators in Thunder Bay were in full swing. There were twenty-eight active elevators on the Thunder Bay waterfront, most working around the clock, and they employed a great many workers. Activity continued after the war and peaked in the 1970s and early 1980s when Thunder Bay elevators shipped seventeen million metric tons of grain a year, thanks largely to the demand for grain coming from the Soviet Union. In 1983, Tom was working in the United Grain Growers elevator. The elevator employed 235 workers operating in three shifts. When he left United Grain Growers in 2010, there were eight workers and the elevator ran only one shift a day.

Herb explained that the decreased elevator operations had led to a corresponding decrease in the local union membership. In the boom time of the early 1980s, there were something like two thousand members of Local 650. The day we met, that number had been "decimated," that is, there were now about two hundred union members working in seven licensed and operating elevators. (The Mission Terminal elevator was also operating, but with a nonunion workforce.)

In the past, most strikes had turned on wage issues. In 1968 there was an eight-week-long strike, and in 1981 a six-week strike.

In 1986, there was a strike that lasted two weeks. By 1991, however, the full effects of the slowdown in elevator operations had been felt, and when Local 650 called a strike, the issues had changed. Since any slowing of grain shipments concerns the Canadian government, the 1991 strike drew the attention of federal politicians. At the invitation of the federal Liberal Party, Herb Daniher was asked to address the Canadian Senate, the upper house of the federal parliament. (The Progressive Conservatives were the governing party at the time and controlled the House of Commons.) Herb went to Ottawa with ten points, none of which asked for a wage increase. He described the issues as "about everything but money"—things such as lowering the retirement age, job security, retraining, and adjusting the pensions of current retirees.

The occasion was serious and ceremonial. When he reached for a water glass before he presented his list of issues, a white-gloved Senate page hurried over and moved the glass closer to his hand. Herb had been prepped by the Liberals for his presentation and was told not to concern himself with the senators in the upper benches, some of whom might be napping. He should direct his attention to those sitting in the front benches in the well of the Senate chamber. The Liberals wanted to know what questions they should ask when he had finished speaking. Herb simply told them, "When you hear what I have to say, you'll know the questions." There was some give and take after Herb spoke, but despite his careful presentation of the complexity of the issues facing workers in Thunder Bay, some senators couldn't get their minds to move beyond old ideas of belligerent wage confrontations between union and management.

The federal government decided that grain shipments had to resume and imposed compulsory arbitration. Local 650 members returned to work and the arbitrator, who had the power to end the strike and impose terms on the parties involved, went about his work. The arbitrator seemed to recast the strike in older, classic terms. He took his time, so that it was 1993 before he delivered his decision. The decision ignored Herb's careful presentation of issues to the Senate. The arbitrator saw the strike as a money issue. He looked at wages for West Coast grain workers and decided that Thunder Bay workers should get a 16 percent wage increase. That might sound good, but it missed the point. In response to the required wage increase, Thunder Bay elevator operators made a further reduction of the local workforce. That was obviously not what the union wanted, but it had proven harder to fight old ideas than management. After the settlement was imposed, the union complained to the International Labour Organization about the Canadian government's actions in the strike and the ILO agreed with the union that the government's actions had breached international labor standards.

Herb told another story that made it clear that it is often hard to get a government representative to overcome his preconceptions and to hear what you are saying. The Lakehead Port Council was making a presentation to a government committee on the sustainability of the St. Lawrence Seaway. One of the committee members was a senator who was a farmer and a member of the Reform Party of Canada. The farmer had obviously brought some historical prejudices against unions to the hearing and when Herb was speaking about union issues at the hearing, the farmer/senator stood up and shouted at Herb that "because of people like you, I ran over my wife with a combine!" Herb was a bit taken aback and decided he had to be careful before he replied. He didn't know, after all, if the angry farmer's wife had lived or died!

8

✦

Transformations

The arc of Buffalo's heady days as a center of grain trading and shipping was long, but it has reached its end. The opening of the St. Lawrence Seaway in 1959 tolled the final bell for Buffalo's terminal elevators. There was no longer any need to unload grain in Buffalo for shipment to points east. The way was clear for large ships from the upper Great Lakes to sail into Lake Ontario and on to other eastern and overseas ports through the improved Welland Canal. The nightmare of Niagara Falls that had long threatened could now be forgotten—except by tourists.

Thunder Bay was among those upper Great Lakes ports that were supposed to benefit from the opening of the St. Lawrence Seaway. For a time, grain shipments did increase because of the demand for grain in the Soviet Union. But as the Soviet Union dissolved and grain production rose in the newly independent countries of Russia and Ukraine, that market disappeared. At the same time, more and more Canadian grain headed west to buyers in the Far East. The obvious result was a reduction in the amount of grain going east via Thunder Bay. Some Thunder Bay elevators had to shut down and were left standing empty.

In Buffalo, terminal elevators became completely superfluous. Soon after the opening of the St. Lawrence Seaway, only three working elevators remained and they didn't send grain on, but received and stored it for local processing. Both Buffalo and Thunder Bay were left with the same question: What do you do with an empty elevator? Often the first thought was to knock it down. That is not easy. Terminal elevators are big and most are made of some combination of brick and reinforced concrete that doesn't give up easily. An elevator can be demolished, of course, but doing it is expensive and money for demolition is scare unless the elevator is standing in the way of a redevelopment project. Initially, pressure for redevelopment in Buffalo was weak. Redevelopment pressure proved to be much stronger in Thunder Bay.

On December 17, 2000, Thunder Bay's Saskatchewan Pool 6 yielded to dynamite. A series of controlled explosions brought it to the ground, as it was leveled to clear the way for a development on the shores of Lake Superior called "Portside." The demolition was a source of local, civic pride. The mayor of Thunder Bay and an alderman pushed down the plunger that set off the explosion. With the prospect of a new development, few regretted the elevator's disappearance. Others, however, thought it a loss.

It's hard to think that demolishing an elevator is a bad idea when someone else has a plan to replace it with something new and shiny, since the likely alternative is not appealing. When an elevator is no longer used as intended and there is no money available for demolition, the elevator tends to go through a slow process of deterioration. Empty elevators soon become abandoned elevators. What was valuable in them is stripped out and sold. Some machines might be reused and, if they can be, the owners of the elevator sell them. But often even that doesn't happen. Anything made of metal can be sold as scrap, including steel bins, if the elevator has any.

Responsible owners may try to find a buyer for the elevator but, more often, the owner walks away leaving the building to be scavenged and graffitied. For some, the abandoned elevator becomes an unofficial urban playground. Most others come to think of it as a large, dangerous eyesore. Local governments often end up owning deserted elevators for nonpayment of taxes, but that just means that they inherit the problem of what to do with them. At that point, the question of what to do with an empty elevator reappears. Should the elevator be demolished or are there other options?

There are options and there are experts ready to suggest them, but they aren't often considered. It is easy to do a roll call of elevators that have disappeared from the landscapes of Buffalo and Thunder Bay. Something makes it easy to demolish elevators without stirring protest. Elevators are big. They are easy to see. But they are usually seen from a distance. And that distance tends to isolate them.

When I was a boy living in Westfort, I didn't have to walk far from my house before I could see the Fort William Elevator. Every time I drove to Port Arthur down the Fort William Road, I could see the row of elevators standing off by the lake. The elevators in the Current River section of Port Arthur also sat beside Lake Superior away from the road. All those elevators were present but separate and at a considerable distance from most peoples' lives.

To get close to the Fort William Elevator, I had to walk over a pedestrian bridge at the end of Brown Street that we called the "Step Bridge." The bridge crossed the CPR railway tracks. Two main-line tracks ran under that bridge and many other tracks filled with railway cars sat in a switching yard beside the main lines. From the middle of the Step Bridge I could see the Paterson Elevator on the Kam River to the right and I could see the Fort William Elevator and other elevators to the left. But even when I got down the steps at the far side of the bridge, it was hard to get to them. I still had to cross a field and make my way over a row of concrete bunkers. You could climb into the bunkers and move around inside from end to end, but they had no evident purpose. I never did learn what they were used for.

I had a similar experience when I went with my father to Manitoba Pool 1 in the intercity area. To get to the elevators, you had to turn off the Fort William Road and drive over a bridge. That bridge crossed another set of railroad tracks that made up the CNR switching yard. The road on the other side of that bridge was rough and untended and ran through fields thick with weeds. The car would bump along this road past the row of intercity elevators until it reached the turn into Pool 1 near its end. In both Westfort and intercity, getting to the elevators felt like a trip away from the city. They were in a place dedicated to work, far away from the part of the city where people lived. Life and work weren't mixed.

It's the same way in Buffalo. The elevators sit south of the downtown area of the city stretched along the Buffalo River and the parallel and even more remote Buffalo Ship Canal. The elevators are at the outer edge of the old First Ward and even, with one exception, stand apart from Lake Eire. The Bazelon photograph at the end of chapter 3 shows some elevators along the Buffalo River making up part of the line of elevators along that river called "Elevator Alley." The name may be appropriate for reasons not intended. The elevators are in the "alley" which means that they are behind and away from the street.

The separation of the elevators from the living spaces of Thunder Bay and Buffalo works on the imagination. They are there, but they are easy to forget. Going to the elevators might seem like a trip to a foreign land. Foreigners are fine but they're different from us. I think that the elevators' foreignness makes it easier to treat them badly. It is at least easier to disregard them.

The Wollenburg Grain and Seed Elevator was a wooden elevator built in Buffalo in 1912. In 2003, local preservationists arranged to have the Wollenburg placed on the National Register of Historic Places. It was a small wooden elevator that could hold only 25,000 bushels of grain. It was long unused, but it represented a rare surviving example of the sort of elevator that was built by Joseph Dart. Over time, its condition had deteriorated and, in the usual course of things, it had come into the hand of the City of Buffalo for nonpayment of property taxes. The city, like most, had other pressing problems to deal with and simply boarded up the doors and windows. Boarding it up didn't prevent the Wollenberg from being entered, vandalized and, eventually, destroyed by an arson fire in October 2006. Being on the National Register didn't save it.

To preserve grain elevators and to save empty elevators from demolition requires bringing them out of their isolation into full attention. It is easy to forget large, imposing buildings if they are imagined to be in a world apart from the daily life of a city. Unused elevators need to be reimagined as part of the city and not left to slip into a ghetto of neglect. Architectural historians have already realized their importance. William Clarkson wrote in his 1981 guide to Buffalo architecture, published by MIT Press, that the Buffalo elevators were a prominent part of "an outdoor museum of extraordinary architecture developed over the one hundred and fifty years of its history." Reyner Banham, in his turn, focused even more attention on Buffalo's elevators in *Concrete Atlantis*. He felt it was a privilege to look down the Buffalo River on the "almost Egyptian monumentality" of the Buffalo elevators. But others need to see the value and beauty of these buildings if they are to survive. It's not enough that they are appreciated by experts or seen solely as museum pieces when their working days are over.

In Buffalo, more and more people are being introduced to the grandeur of the elevators through the Buffalo River History Tours. Queen City Ferry Company operates a tour boat that makes daily trips down the river to show off the wonders of Elevator Alley, Silo City, and the Concrete Central elevator. The trip begins at the Commercial Slip right at the spot where the Erie Canal terminated. Ric Hilliman runs the tours and also captains the *Spirit of Buffalo*, a sailing yacht that takes passengers out of Buffalo harbor for a cruise on Lake Erie. Ric's business has grown with the renewal of the Buffalo waterfront. Many more Buffalonians and visitors to the city now come to the waterfront area. There is a new Naval Park there with three Navy ships open for tours and, if you look closely, you can see a plaque showing the place where Dart's elevator stood. You can sit in a restaurant on the waterfront and look across the mouth of the Buffalo River and out into Lake Erie. Across the river to the left is the Connecting Terminal elevator, the first in the string of elevators that line the Buffalo River and the ship canal.

The renewed waterfront is reconnecting Buffalonians to elements of its industrial past. It has overcome the remoteness of the elevators in particular, and opens minds to the ways that the elevators many be brought into the life of the city. Buffalo's Naval Park seems to be the first step in a revitalization process that will carry on down the river and reconnect with areas of the old First Ward that many of the citizens of Buffalo, other than those who live in the First Ward, have never visited. The hope is that the process will lead to the preservation of Buffalo's grain elevators. Demolition of an elevator is the ultimate form of disregard, but many will be demolished if they are not widely seen as a valuable element in the future of the city.

Fortunately, a second life for abandoned elevators is possible. That life can take one of three forms: reuse, preservation, or transformation. Reuse is easy to imagine, but hard to effect. Preservation and transformation are harder and each has its own special problems.

Some elevators do survive to work again. The United Grain Growers elevator in Thunder Bay became the Viterra "C" House and then sat unused for two years until purchased by the Richardson Company, whose elevator sits beside it on the Lake Superior waterfront. It is now being put back into use as part of the Richardson Elevator complex in Thunder Bay. In Buffalo, the Lake and Rail Elevator came to life again in an involved, two-step process. ConAgra owned a group of three elevators, all of which were out of use. It isn't easy to sell a nonworking grain elevator, so it was no surprise that when Rick Smith expressed interest in the ConAgra property, the ConAgra president quickly traveled to Buffalo. Rick was not looking to buy an elevator. He just wanted to acquire an easement across the ConAgra land. ConAgra's president suggested to Rick that he go beyond his easement idea and buy the ConAgra land and all three of the elevators on it. ConAgra's desire to sell suited a plan that was in Rick's mind, so he made an offer to ConAgra that was accepted and the sale was completed in April 2006.

Rick planned to put together a group of investors interested in building an ethanol plant on the site. Ethanol is made from corn and the elevators on the site had plenty of capacity to hold the corn needed for production. But the ethanol plan went awry. Nearby residents complained and by the time their complaints were dealt with, the ethanol market had changed in ways that made it unprofitable to proceed. Rick's group had begun to prepare one of the elevators, the Lake and Rail Elevator, to receive and handle corn, so it was on its way to being ready to be used again. It was no longer needed to store corn, but it could store grain, and Whitebox Commodities took advantage of the opportunity. Whitebox is a commodities futures company that buys and holds grain for future sale when the markets are right, and the Lake and Rail represents only one among many elevators that Whitebox has acquired.

Under Whitebox's ownership, the Lake and Rail again functions as an elevator. Grain has been brought to the elevator both by rail and by lake boat. In September 2008, the 690-foot *American Fortitude* delivered four hundred thousand bushels of wheat to the elevator, proving that the Buffalo River could still handle large ships, even as far up the river as the Lake and Rail. The elevator continues to operate today. But finding a way for an elevator to work again as originally intended isn't easy. Usually, the puzzle of what to do with an empty elevator is much harder to solve.

Rick Smith, in the meantime, bought another elevator located close to the three elevators he had purchased from ConAgra. A City of Buffalo employee had bought the Marine A elevator at an auction sale, and in August 2006, Rick Smith bought it from him and added it to the other elevators he owned. After the sale of the Lake and Rail, Rick was left with a cluster of three elevators. Rick is perhaps one of the few people with the energy and imagination to have seen this situation as an opportunity. He envisioned the possibility of the three elevators becoming a site for exciting new uses. The idea of "Silo City" as a performance and exhibition space and a place for industrial innovation was born. The full story is worth telling, but it needs some additional background and a buildup to be completely appreciated.

Preservation: Problems and Promises

The Friends of Grain Elevators in Thunder Bay have a preservation plan that is as close to pure as possible. They want to gain historic status for the Western 10 Elevator in the Westfort area of Thunder Bay and make it accessible to visitors who want to know how a grain elevator works. Getting the elevator on the Canadian Historic Register would help in raising funds to create an exhibition site at the elevator and to develop tours and displays promoting the grain handling industry. The Friends of Grain Elevators have made the

Western 10 Elevator a candidate for designation as a "national historic site." The process of applying to the National Historic Sites and Monuments Board is underway and an architect from the board has already toured the elevator as one of the first steps toward awarding historic status.

The Western 10 Elevator faces some problems. It is on the Kaministiquia River, and lake boats and oceangoing ships now have a hard time navigating the river. The river has not been dredged in a while and the boats have become bigger. Bigger boats mean deeper draughts and, hence, the need for a deeper channel in the river and deeper slips at the elevator. The net result is that boats can't take on a full load at Western 10. At best, they can take a half-load, but those willing to do so are few. Oceangoing ships are the ones most likely to make their way up the Kam to the elevator because they sometimes need a partial load of "specialty grains." The elevator's owner, Maurice Mailhot, has worked hard to carve out a niche business in this area and in other grains outside mainstream distribution. When I was in Thunder Bay recently, the *Jan S* was docked beside Western 10 taking on a half-load of lentils. After loading at Western, the captain planned to travel down the river to the Mission Terminal elevator to complete its load and then set sail with his Romanian crew for Turkey.

Other Thunder Bay elevators handle lentils, but it's unusual. They are not, properly speaking, a specialty grain. That category includes canary seed and three different kinds of mustard seed. Western 10 has handled canary seed and, at one time, bagged it and sent it by rail to Mexico. But that business has fallen off. Western also handles identity-preserved or "IP" grain. IP grain has to be kept separate from other grains through the whole delivery system from farmer to consumer. Buyers of organic wheat or soybeans want to be sure that they are getting their products from farms that have been certified "organic" and that no other grain has been mixed with it on its way from the farm. Growers International in Winnipeg inspects elevators and grants certification to those who qualify to handle IP grain. Western 10 has that certification and knows how to segregate IP grain and to ensure that it has been handled correctly on its way to market. Handling IP grain is important to Western's business and it may become more important to all of the Thunder Bay elevators.

Western's circumstances have made it unnecessary to invest in new equipment and methods. It is able to carry on its business without having had to change the way it operates. This means that the elevator runs in a way that makes it even more appealing to the Friends of Grain Elevators. Its methods of grain handling are closer to earlier methods and its equipment is of the sort that has not been updated or replaced in the way it has in other Thunder Bay elevators. For example, unlike the Richardson elevator, Western 10's scales are at the top of the elevator, above the distribution floor where they always used to be. There are even still some rope-driven pulleys powering wooden-toothed gears in the elevator that delight older elevators workers who have toured the Western elevator and been reminded of the ways elevators used to work. The combination of limited operations and more traditional methods is attractive to a group that wants to preserve and exhibit a more traditional form of elevator operation.

If Western 10 gets historic status the Friends of Grain elevators can work with Maurice Mailhot on a plan to open the elevator to visitors so that they can see the workings of an elevator at first hand.

It is a bold plan that could help to keep the elevator in operation and also allow people to see how it works. Thunder Bay has a thriving tourist industry. Lake Superior draws many visitors. The area's summers may be short, but they are very pleasant and the U.S. border is only about fifty miles away. Duluth is within easy reach and Minneapolis is within a day's drive. Large numbers already come to visit the reconstructed Fort William on the upper Kam River where life in fur trading days is reenacted. The Friends of Grain Elevators think that grain handling has its own romance and could draw visitors as well—perhaps even the same visitors who come to see the fur trading fort.

The Friends of Grain Elevators' plan incorporates ideas familiar to preservationists and urban architectural planners: "adaptive reuse" and "industrial tourism." These ideas promote reusing old industrial sites—making them attractive and interesting so that people want to visit. Many sites have been preserved in this way. There is a jute mill in Dundee, Scotland, that offers a tour to visitors. The mill has the same machinery it did when it was turning jute fibers into cloth in the nineteenth century. Talking models reproduce the sorts of conversations you might have heard on the mill floor and office. My grandmother Tarbet was a "Dundee weaver"—one of the many young girls who came into Dundee to work in the jute mills. They came to Dundee because women would work in the mills for a salary that men refused to accept and many a man in Dundee stayed home to do the cooking and look after the "wee ans" rather than take the low wage their wives worked for.

There are many more industrial sites and manmade objects that have been preserved and the number is growing, but nothing has equaled the Duisburg Nord Landscape Park in Germany. The park is a primary inspiration for Lynda Schneekloth and others from the School of Architecture and Planning at the University of Buffalo who want to preserve and reuse the Buffalo elevators. The Duisburg park was designed in 1991 by Peter Latz and has converted a massive coal and steel production complex in the Ruhr River valley from an industrial wasteland into a vast public park. The park is on the Emscher River, which had been described as an "industrial sewer" because of the coal, steel, and chemical industries that lined its banks. Yet despite the environmental challenges that this site presented to him, Latz had the imagination to see beyond industrial grime to a vision of a regional leisure and arts center. Slag heaps became display mounts for sculpture, steel mills became concert halls and gas tanks became swimming pools. There are walking and bicycling paths through and around industrial remains and chemical landfills were either capped or remediated by plantings that covered, and will eventually eliminate, the environmental dangers.

The key decision in Duisburg was to leave the industrial structures in place. The buildings, cranes, bridges, and machines used in industry evoke the memory of their past use like nothing else. That historical value is what preservationists want to maintain. Clearing a site of the structures that once occupied it clears it of its past associations and, while all that is past is not precious, what is precious disappears with the buildings if they are removed. To quote Lynda Schneekloth, "You can't tell the story if you haven't got the goods," and for her and her associates in Buffalo the goods are the elevator buildings themselves.

Lynda edited the 2007 collection of essays called, *Reconsidering Concrete Atlantis: Buffalo Grain Elevators*. It is a wonderful collection containing both a historical account of the Buffalo elevators and imaginative ideas for their reuse. The architecture students who contributed plans and ideas to this collection all knew one thing—that the elevator structures themselves are fundamental to preserving the history of grain handling in Buffalo. Without them, the "goods" go missing.

The Duisburg park was a remarkable accomplishment that would be harder to duplicate in Buffalo. There was political will in Germany to solve an unemployment crisis and to build the park to alleviate that problem. That political will committed large amounts of public money to the project. New York State has also committed public money to renewing Buffalo's waterfront, but no one expects it to match the money needed to create a Duisburg-like park in Buffalo. Transformation in Buffalo will be more incremental and will have to involve private, as well as public, investment.

Many possibilities for a transformation have already been laid out in Lynda Schneekloth's collection. There is a map of a land and water grain elevator heritage trail that could be implemented without any alteration of the exiting elevators. They would become the background for a series of areas open for recreation that would involve sowing grain and herbs and planting fruit trees on the vacant land between the elevators as well as providing open fields for active recreation. More ambitious plans have been imagined by other contributors: a moving track through elevator bins, a music center inside the Peavey elevator, and a performance stage inside the Electric Elevator Annex. They may not be very practical, but the entertainment they would provide answers the question that Michael Frisch poses in the title of his essay, "Where Is the Fun in a Grain Elevator?" It would require revenue from many visitors to justify creation of this transformed world, but two to three million people visit Niagara Falls each year. Maybe some could be persuaded to make the short trip to Buffalo if such a fanciful creation drew them in.

Things are already happening. A plan is underway to light the Ohio Street Bridge, which is in the middle of Buffalo's Elevator Alley. A developer plans to transform the abandoned Wheeler-GLF elevator into a brewery, entertainment, and recreation center. There is a plan to project a spectacle on the bins of the Connecting Terminal elevator. A Montreal-based group, Ambiant Design Productions, will install and present the show based on a similar presentation in Quebec City called the Aurora Borealis Project. The show is expected to be a major tourist attraction that will use contemporary art to highlight Buffalo's industrial past and showcase the elevators in particular. The Erie Canal Harbor Development Corp. has already voted the funding for the light show, which could herald many similar projects to use and transform the elevators of Buffalo. In Silo City, crowds have already been drawn to events there that have included an outdoor art show and the Torn Space Theater's multimedia performances. And there is more to come.

9

Grain Dust Dreams

I first heard about Silo City from Judy Slater, a Buffalo friend. When I told her about my interest in the Buffalo elevators, she suggested that I come to Buffalo for a tour. Beth Tauke, the associate dean of the School of Architecture and Planning at the University of Buffalo and an enthusiast for the preservation of the Buffalo elevators, offered to give a tour of Marine A, and I was happy to join in. We were a mixed group, including friends from my days in Buffalo and others who had heard about the elevator visit one way or another. Beth knows Marine A well and has brought her students and enthusiasts to the elevator many times.

Marine A is one of the elevators acquired by Rick Smith and it had already taken on a new life. A string quartet had performed a concert of John Cage music under an open bin in the basement of the elevator. The audience sat in a circle around the musicians and the music bounced and reverberated inside the full height of the open bin. John Cage would have loved the effect, and the performance of his music in such an interesting space was a fitting tribute to a composer of experimental music who had composed and performed some of his most daring works when he taught in the music department of the University of Buffalo.

On the day we made the tour, Marine A housed an exhibit of artwork by some of Beth's students. A stingray-shaped form the color of concrete and pierced with holes spread out under a bin at the far end of the elevator basement. Above and beside it were strings of what looked like Ping-Pong balls hanging down from the roof.

Despite the art displays, you could still imagine the way the elevator looked when it was in use. We entered the roomy basement of the elevator building through an opening in one end and looked down a long line of metal funnels hanging from the bottom of the now-empty bins. The main conveyor belt that once ran under the bins was gone. Rusted remains from the conveyor were tumbled in piles near the basement walls, but it was apparent where they had been. The floors had been swept clean but the walls were dotted with graffiti images and slogans left by urban adventurers who had visited after the elevator had been abandoned. The bottoms of some of the bins were open and you could duck inside the funnel bottoms and look up through the opening for one hundred feet to the bin tops. Light came in through windows on both sides of the basement and rusted and broken stairs appeared occasionally running up to doors that would lead outside, if they could be opened. When we went outside to the dock area, the elevator's rusted marine leg still sat on rails that ran along the dock. The youngest member of our party climbed up into it for a better view of the Buffalo River.

Marine A is part of a cluster of four elevators that includes the American (also known as the Peavey), Perot Malting, and the Lake and Rail. They surround an open space with a hut inhabited by the spirit of the place and the unofficial mayor of Silo City, Swannie Jim. Jim had been there to welcome us before our tour of Marine A and, when that tour ended, he took us on a tour of Perot Malting. A malt house such as the Perot prepares and stores malted barley for use in brewing beer. It was last operated for that purpose by the Fred Koch brewing company. The malt house itself is an attractive brick building built a bit away from the water. It has no marine leg, because it doesn't need one. A conveyor belt runs to the bins of Perot Malting from the bins of the nearby American Elevator. This conveyor supplied Perot Malting with the barley it used.

Much of the equipment in the malt house remains in good shape and there has been talk of its getting back into the malting business. If it doesn't, its interior space looks like it could accommodate a hip, stylish restaurant. It even has a great view. From the open end on the top floor of the malt house, you can see over the railway tracks to the Buffalo River and farther on to an impressive row of elevators lining the river.

By the time we had finished our tour of Marine A and Perot Malting it was late afternoon and we had gathered again in front of Jim's hut. As we talked, a dark green 1973 Oldsmobile convertible with the top down drove along Childs Street and pulled up beside our group. The driver was as notable as the car. He wore a cowboy hat and sported a prominent mustache. When he stepped out of the car, we could see the cowboy boots that complemented the hat. This was my introduction to Rick Smith: businessman, entrepreneur, and the owner of Silo City.

That first meeting with Rick impressed me, but I didn't get much chance to talk to him until about a year later. We sat in his office at Rigidized Metals. I reminded him that the Silo City elevators had come to him pretty much by chance. The sale from ConAgra wasn't planned and the difficulties with the ethanol idea that had developed after the sale had not been anticipated. RiverWright Energy, the group Rick had put together to undertake ethanol production, had not lasted. He consequently held title to a set of elevators with no apparent use. I asked him if that had been discouraging.

That wasn't Rick's reaction, and as we talked I began to see how he had been able to keep on looking for the next opportunity. Those elevators represented the confluence of two different currents in Rick Smith's life. One branch flowed from the world of business. Rigidized Metals had been founded by Rick's grandfather in 1940 with the purpose of designing and manufacturing metal needed to build aircraft. Both Bell Helicopter and Curtiss-Wright built aircraft in Buffalo and there was a heavy demand for their products, especially in the years after the United States joined World War II. By embossing a pattern on uniformly thin metal, Rigidized Metals produced just the sort of material that the aircraft industry wanted—light, flexible, and strong. The business flourished and Rick's grandfather carried it on for many years. It was not until 1968, when Rick was seven years old, that his father took over and Rick's father and mother moved the family from Cleveland to Buffalo. Family businesses often don't stay in the family for more than two generations and, for a time, it looked as if that would be the case for Rigidized Metals.

Rick went to a fine private school in Buffalo and on to the University of Pennsylvania, and it looked like his life was on a different course from his father's and grandfather's. After university, Rick went to South Africa to be a musician, and when he returned to the United States it was as a squash pro in Denver. He didn't get back to Buffalo until 1998 when he was thirty-eight years old. And he did not return to join the Rigidized Metals Company. He returned to do what he had to do to help his family. If his mother had not become ill, he might not have joined the business at all. His father needed to look after his mother, and that meant that someone else—Rick—had to look after Rigidized Metals. Things moved fast, and almost before he could think about whether he wanted to do the job long-term, Rick was the president and COI.

Rick had become a businessman and his business was running successfully, but the other current in his life flowed from a different source. That source was music and the world of performance, and it had left its mark. As I talked to Rick, he kept coming up with exciting and original ideas—the sort of ideas more likely to come from an artist. When he talked about the elevators in Silo City, preservation was not the first thing on his mind. As he put it, "Preservation is great, but we are more about regeneration." He could see Silo City in innovative ways. Part of it could foster discovery. The American Elevator could become a campus where students and engineers developed new construction materials. Those new materials might, in turn, lead to new building designs. Marine A could become even more of an exhibition and performance space. Perot Malting could house a stylish restaurant.

Such ideas went together easily in his mind. For Rick, "Design is always centered in the arts," so the natural complement to a materials and design lab would be music and visual arts. The renovations to the

American and Marine A would, at a deeper level, be a combination. Rick is at ease with such notions because he's got the looseness of a former rock musician who "doesn't want to master plan this to death." These development ideas are his, but anyone with other ideas for using Silo City is welcome to propose them. Rick is ready to listen.

This may not be the perfect attitude for the serious preservationist, but, in the United States, where reuse of older industrial buildings is more likely to come from private, rather than public, funding sources, this may be the most workable. When Rick stops to look at the ideas that have guided the regeneration of Buffalo, he sees two that are underway and imagines Silo City supplying the third. In downtown Buffalo, there is a movement to make the city more "livable." Apartments are being built, shops are opening, and the major cultural institutions such as the Albright-Knox Art Gallery and Kleinhans Music Hall are putting their best foot forward. South of the city, the Larkenville area is concentrating on featuring Buffalo as a center for "work."

In 1904, John Larkin commissioned Frank Lloyd Wright to design an office building for the Larkin Soap Company. The Larkin Company was a very successful national mail order business whose principals included, along with Larkin himself, Elbert Hubbard and Darwin Martin. The building, constructed in 1906, was revolutionary. It was made of red sandstone and yellow brick and, although its two-hundred-foot-high exterior was forbidding, inside it had a light-filled open space stretching from floor to glass ceiling. Completely air-conditioned, it incorporated special materials to absorb sound and cushion the steps of workers. Between its support pillars were fourteen sets of three inspirational words, likely contributed by Hubbard. They included such combinations as: GENEROSITY ALTRUISM SACRIFICE; INTEGRITY LOYALTY FIDELITY; IMAGINATION JUDGEMENT INITIATIVE; INTELLIGENCE ENTHUSIASM CONTROL; CO-OPERATION ECONOMY INDUSTRY. They were meant to encourage enterprise, and appeared right across from the workers' desks. The Larkin Building became a model workplace whose design was widely copied. Today, it's a parking lot. The building was demolished in 1950. It is remembered today in tours that regret its loss.

To the themes of "living" and "working," Rick wants Silo City to add "fun." For him, the secret to Buffalo's rebirth lies in keeping and attracting people in their twenties to the city. Many move away from Buffalo and few replace them. Those who do move to Buffalo come to love the city and the Western New York area and are often the prime movers behind the preservation of Buffalo's past. An article in the November 6, 2013, edition of the *New York Times* talks about the opportunities available to young developers in the low-cost housing stock of Buffalo. This article, "Small-Scale Developers, Big Dreams," describes the "young hipsters" who are attracted to the city and who are happily restoring houses there.

Others have come to Buffalo to teach in its colleges and at the university. They also support efforts at urban renewal. The university's Architecture School has certainly focused attention on the beauty and value of the Buffalo elevators. But Rick feels that the serious-minded professionals, such as those who come to teach, need to be supplemented by those like the "hipsters" mentioned in the *New York Times* who come because it is fun and exciting to live in Buffalo. Music and art are a part of the attraction, but activities such as biking, kayaking, and rock climbing are more likely to prompt people to explore and enjoy the city. One of the bins at Marine A is already being converted into a rock climbing center on both the inside and outside of the bin. There will be bikes and kayaks to rent on the river near the elevator and the restaurant idea for Perot Malting has already stirred some interest.

These things aren't Rick's work alone. Others are working to make them happen. The Buffalo Niagara Riverkeepers, along with the area's local congressman, Brian Higgins, have put in the time and money needed to clean up the Buffalo River. The Riverkeepers run both biking and paddling tours of the man-made canyons that the grain elevators have created along the Buffalo River, and the Buffalo Scholastic Rowing Association has set up the headquarters for its rowing club on Ohio Street right beside the Buffalo River. No one is swimming in the river yet, but that may be coming soon. Recreation on the Buffalo River is one of the "strange and unexpected inheritances" of the Buffalo grain elevators. If the elevators had not been located on the river, the river would have remained largely inaccessible. The mouth of the river was blocked by sandbars that made it difficult to navigate and it had to be dredged to make the entrance deep enough for lake boats to get their grain cargoes to the elevators built along its banks. Now the river is there to use.

I left Rigidized Metals with Rick Smith's unusual embossed metal business card in my pocket and a renewed desire to visit Silo City. I headed back down Ohio Street and turned into Childs Street heading toward Swannie Jim's hut. As I did, I drove past a strange structure on my right. It was a twenty-two-foot-high tower of hexagon-shaped metal plates. The metal plates were silver colored and pierced with irregular triangular holes whose use was later explained by Swannie Jim. The tower, as it turns out, is a beehive, the result of a competition that Rick Smith promoted among architecture students at the University of Buffalo. When first working on the elevators he had purchased, Rick discovered a large hive of bees. Rather than exterminate them, he decided to give them a new and impressive home. The new home, now amusingly called "Elevator B" has been a great success. It was built, the bees moved in, and, to everyone's delight, they liked it. Their honey-making activity is impressive. It is hard to imagine what the hive looks like, but you can see it at: http: www.fastcoexist.com/1680215/a-gorgeous-towering-hive-to-save-our-dying-bees#1. It's more evidence of the imagination that Rick Smith and the University of Buffalo have brought to the revitalization of the Silo City space.

Farther down the road, Jim was sitting outside his hut beside Marine A. Beside him was his loud, large, and, despite appearances, gentle dog. It was a cool but sunny late April afternoon and sitting outside was comfortable. Swannie Jim is hard to categorize. When I asked Rick Smith to describe Jim's role, it was one of the few times he had to hesitate before he answered. He finally came up with the title of the "steward" of Silo City, but he immediately moved away from Jim's job description to listing his personal qualities. "Well-read, knowledgeable, curious," were some of the words he used. All that is true, but you have to talk to Jim to realize it. He doesn't care much for the outward signs of status. In fact, I'd say he doesn't really give a damn. His jacket was torn; his baseball cap showed the signs of hard wear, but he looked completely comfortable—as if he had found his perfect spot in Silo City.

I asked Jim to describe himself, and the best that he could come up with was that he was a "mechanic." Even that wasn't simple. By "mechanic," he meant that "if you are at A and want to get to B, and if people tell you there is no way to get there, I might be able to help." And being a mechanic hardly fits with his education and background. He went to college to study fine art (drawing and ceramics) and his last formal job was working as an "engineer" on plant construction for National Gypsum, although he had no formal training as an engineer; he just knew how to do the job.

Everyone knows him as "Swannie Jim," but his proper name is Jim Watkins. He came to Buffalo in 2001 with some savings but no job and decided to take time off to build a boat. He rented a small building on the Buffalo River and got to work. When I asked him to explain how he got the "Swannie" nickname, he said that every boatbuilder has a "groaning chair"—a chair he can sit in holding his head when something in the boatbuilding process inevitably goes wrong and needs to be thought over. Jim didn't have such a chair in his workshop, but The Swannie House's forty barstools were a short walk away. He spent a lot of time in The Swannie House puzzling through his boatbuilding problems while using one of the barstools as his groaning chair. It was there that he met Rick Smith. When Rick came into The Swannie House in his trademark cowboy hat and boots, Jim was curious about how someone dressed like that was in Buffalo rather than Texas or Wyoming. The bar owner thought the two of them would like one another and introduced them. Since Jim's work on building his Bristol Channel–style boat was slowing and his pockets were, in his words, "running short," the meeting was fortunate for both. Jim needed work and Rick needed someone he could depend on to keep an eye on Silo City.

Jim has settled into the job—whatever it may be. He seems to be content and at ease with his role—whatever it is. He has absorbed the history of Buffalo, especially of the First Ward, and knows the details of the elevators' history and construction as few others do.

He seems almost to have adopted them as his own. Former elevator workers come to visit him, students from the university want to talk to him about them, and preservationists like Lynda Schneekloth and Beth Tauke mention him in their first breath when they talk about the elevators.

He got his nickname because of his well-known association with The Swannie House and he also knows the story of how The Swannie House got its name. The Swannie House has been operating for a long time and, as the oldest surviving waterfront bar, is closely connected to the dusty-throated elevator workers who worked nearby. In the 1920s, a Polish family named Swinerski bought the bar but found that the Irish controlled the distribution of liquor and beer in the First Ward. No distributor would deal with them if they gave the bar their family name. The closest they could come was to call it The Swannie House and that, apparently, was good enough to get them admitted to the trade.

The First Ward is known for its bars. Jim also talked about McCarthy's Pub and the central role that Gene McCarthy played in the ward. He was as famous for bookmaking as for his support of the local Little League teams, and McCarthy's Pub stood in a long line of establishments known to elevator workers that stretched back to the days when bar owners controlled the hiring of "scoopers" to unload grain from the lake boats that pulled alongside the Buffalo elevators.

Of course, those days are gone, as was all too clear as Jim and I sat and talked. Not far from us was a pickup truck with a working generator in back. It was powering the tools being used to create the climbing site for Silo City Rocks in one of the Marine A bins. The boat going by on the river was a Scholastic Rowing Club eight, not a grain carrier. The Lake and Rail was operating and you could still smell grain dust, but the clouds of grain dust were gone. But Marine A still stood tall, Perot Malting looked handsome in the sun, and the American Elevator behind us looked suitably distinguished because of its recent entry on the National Register of Historic Places. The old dust clouds were giving way to new grain dust dreams.

On my next visit to Buffalo, I decided to visit The Swannie House as a tribute to Jim. There are many good reasons to visit. The beer is great, the meals are hearty, and the attitude is welcoming and easy, but its location is a special bonus. The front door faces Ohio Street, the street that runs along the Buffalo River. It is on a corner, the corner of Ohio and Michigan, right where the Michigan Street Bridge crosses the river. Go there on a sunny day when the wind is blowing in from Lake Erie. Stand out front and take a deep breath. The General Mills elevator is just across the bridge and it makes a whole lot of Cheerios every day. The smell of fresh-baked Cheerios is delightful. It might be one of the best free attraction in the city.

Afterword

Talking to friends and acquaintances about writing this book was interesting. Their first reaction was almost always puzzlement. But, as I described grain elevators, they discovered that the subject had unexpected charms. Some remembered their encounters with these large and imposing structures and recalled the impressions they had left. Others became curious and began to ask questions.

One friend emailed me from Kansas. He was driving across country and marveled at how he could gauge the distance between towns by the appearance of the next elevator on the horizon. A hospital worker I talked to in Boston got a dreamy look in her eyes as she remembered the elevators that were constant companions to her childhood in Alberta. Once recalled or once brought to consciousness, most wondered how elevators came to be and everyone wanted to know how they worked.

There are other books on grain elevators—many others. Most concentrate on how they look. Elevators are fascinating subjects for photographers and painters. Sometimes, as in Charles Demuth's *My Egypt*, on the cover of this book, they symbolize energy and power. They are North America's challengers to the glory of the Egyptian pyramids. Sometimes they stir profound emotions. The picture of a prairie elevator against a dark evening sky evokes feelings of isolation and loneliness. Sometimes the photos suggest perseverance and shabby nobility. My brother-in-law, Tom Houlihan, when he heard I was writing this book, sent me an elegiac photo of a Chicago elevator, rusting, discolored, and unused.

The Buffalo elevators continue to fascinate photographers. Silo City now sponsors an annual Photography Workshop that focuses on creating images of the Buffalo elevators.

In 1999, the German photographer Gerritt Engel produced an impressive book of photographs called *Buffalo Grain Elevators*. Michael Cook's 2010 book *Elevator Alley* is generously illustrated with photos of the Buffalo elevators by Andrew Emond. In 2011, Bruce Jackson's photos of the Buffalo elevators were exhibited in a show called *American Chartres*. The exhibit was reviewed by Lynda Schneekloth in the January 19, 2011, issue of *Artvoice* magazine. That review includes an interview with Jackson. In it, he reveals the powerful attraction that elevators, particularly the Buffalo elevators, have for a photographer.

Reyner Banham recruited the photographer Patricia Layman Bazelon to assist him in refocusing attention on the Buffalo elevators in his book, *A Concrete Atlantis*. Her photographs of Buffalo's elevators are unforgettable. They have been collected by Buffalo's CEPA Gallery in a display entitled *Grain Elevators and Steel: Architectural Photography of Buffalo* that is available online. The elevator photos in this collection are archetypal images of the beauty and dignity of elevator architecture.

Many other books display images of elevators located throughout the United States and Canada. I understand the attraction that grain elevators hold for photographers. The books and exhibitions that picture them deserve attention and praise. But I have taken a different approach. If I had to analogize elevators to humans and imagine elevators as having bodies and roles, I wouldn't see them as photographic models—attractive as they are. I would see them as workers.

Terminal elevators have a job to do. Grain is one of life's staples. Whether grain is fed to animals or processed into cereals, flour, or pasta, it is fundamental to the food that sustains us. Few of us live on farms or near the land where grain is grown. Grain, therefore, has to be moved in large quantities over great distances to get to the creatures that consume it. Moving that grain is a Herculean task, and terminal elevators are the colossi that perform it. They stand in the middle of a deep river of grain that flows toward them. They lift, sort, and send on that grain so that the river of grain flows on to reach all of us.

I admire the job that terminal elevators do and marvel at how wonderfully they perform it. But don't be taken in by my metaphor. The work of a grain elevator is done by real workers. They are the ones who deserve our admiration, even though they would be surprised by the attention. In spite of the dangers and difficulties, they show up daily to do a hard job and think themselves happy to have it.

If you haven't thought about what that job involves, I hope this book has brought it to mind. Perhaps you will recover a memory of grain elevators you've known, or discover that there is more to terminal grain elevators than you had ever imagined.

Index